Lifesavers
for
Substitutes

A Wealth of Ideas for the Classroom Teacher as Well

by
Mary McMillan

illustrated by Vanessa Filkins

Cover by Vanessa Filkins

ISBN No. 0-86653-678-7

Good Apple
A Division of Frank Schaffer Publication, Inc.
23740 Hawthorne Boulevard
Torrance, CA 90505-5927

Table of Contents

GA1412

GA1412

Introduction

Rules to follow to become a great sub:

Rule 1: Come prepared! Never come to a classroom empty handed. Most teachers will leave wonderful lesson plans for substitute teachers to follow; however, there are those occasions when a teacher is called off duty on an emergency or becomes suddenly ill and is unable to leave things in perfect order. My suggestion is to carry a semi-large cloth bag in which to carry backup ideas, supplies, handout papers, etc., into the classroom with you. Be prepared! Be a bag lady!

Rule 2: Keep them busy and learning at the same time! You will find that if the children are kept busy, they will have fewer opportunities to misbehave with their teacher away. You will experience more successful results if the children are given activities that are valid learning exercises. Children never respond well to "busy work." They like to be challenged to learn with exciting, fun ideas such as those found throughout this book. Keep them busy! Keep them learning!

Rule 3: Be on your toes! Even the best of students become adventuresome when the teacher is away. Let the students know right away that you are in charge and that you have things under control. Bringing in backup activities and being prepared is one way to show the students just how in control you are.

Most teachers will leave you names of students that you can depend on for cooperation with needed questions. If not, ask the other grade level teachers for assistance. They are there for you and want to be relied upon if needed. Otherwise, they will simply let you do your job your way unless they recognize some trouble spot that needs attention. Remember, be on your toes! Let the students know right from the start that you are in control and in charge of the situation.

Rule 4: Inform the teacher! A teacher appreciates a note written by the substitute letting him know how the day went. Most appreciated comments are the positive ones! Start with those!

If you use some of the ideas and activities from this book, share them with the teacher and let him/her know how they worked. But be careful! The teacher just might copy some of the ideas!

Follow the rules. Keep the teacher informed, and you will probably be asked back again and again!

GA1412

First Things First

Before you can begin to walk into a classroom situation, a substitute teacher needs to have access to certain information in order to carry out the plans for the day.

Pertinent information includes a class list; a daily schedule; routine procedures including attendance, lunch count and recess; emergency procedures; students with special needs; students with special classes; students with reliable information; special instructions and, of course, lesson plans.

The following pages provide you with forms for gathering such information.

Substitute teachers need to keep teachers informed as well. The following form provides space on which to write a note to the classroom teacher informing him/her of how well the day went and of any significant information concerning certain students.

GA1412

For Subs Only

DAILY SCHEDULE

TIME	SUBJECT	SPECIAL INSTRUCTIONS

ABC Routine Procedures 123

OPENING:

ATTENDANCE:

LUNCH COUNT:

RECESS:

NOON:

DISMISSAL:

CLASS LIST

1. _____
2. _____
3. _____
4. _____
5. _____
6. _____
7. _____
8. _____
9. _____
10. _____
11. _____
12. _____
13. _____
14. _____
15. _____
16. _____
17. _____
18. _____
19. _____
20. _____
21. _____
22. _____
23. _____
24. _____
25. _____

GA1412

SPECIAL
INSTRUCTIONS FOR THE SUB

STUDENTS WITH SPECIAL NEEDS

1. _____

_____

2. _____

3. _____

4. _____

5. _____

EMERGENCY PROCEDURES

FIRE DRILL:

BAD WEATHER DRILL:

NURSE'S SCHEDULE:

FIRST-AID TIPS:

SPECIFIC TIPS FOR HANDLING DISCIPLINE PROBLEMS:

STUDENTS WITH SPECIAL CLASSES

NAME	CLASS	DAY/TIME
1.		
2.		
3.		
4.		
5.		
6.		
7.		
8.		

STUDENTS WITH RELIABLE INFORMATION

1. _____

2. _____

3. _____

4. _____

5. _____

GA1412

Day-by-Day Lesson Plans for Substitute Teacher

Reproduce as many lesson plan sheets as needed per day for a substitute teacher. Fill out and add to your daily lesson plan book for additional instructions other than those previously made.

Lesson Plans for Substitute Teacher

A+A+A+A+A+A+A+A+A+A+A+A+A+A+A+A+A+A+A+A+A+A+A+A+A+A+A+A+A+A+A+A+A+A+A+A+A+A+A+

Name of school _____

Teacher's name _____

Substitute teacher's name _____

Date _____ Day of the week _____

A+A+A+A+A+A+A+A+A+A+A+A+A+A+A+A+A+A+A+A+A+A+A+A+A+A+A+A+A+A+A+A+A+A+A+A+A+A+A+

TIME	SUBJECT/ACTIVITY	LESSON PLANS

GA1412

More Lesson Plans for Substitute Teacher

A+A+A+A+A+A+A+A+A+A+A+A+A+A+A+A+A+A+A+A+A+A+A+A+A+A+A+A+A+A+A+A+A+A+A+A+A+A+A+A+A+

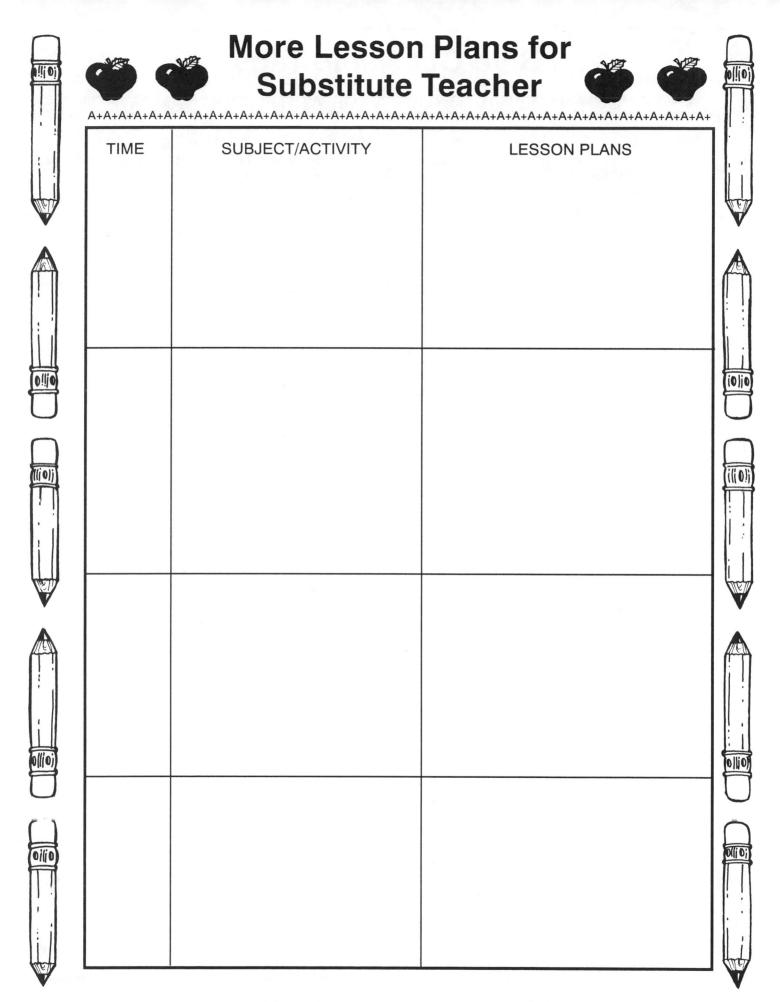

TIME	SUBJECT/ACTIVITY	LESSON PLANS

GA1412

Give Out Name Tags

WRITE YOUR NAME WRITE YOUR NAME WRITE YOUR NAME WRITE

Name tags help substitute teachers in any grade. Reproduce the following patterns by running off as many name tags as needed for the classroom. Have the students color, cut out and write their own names and any other information required on the tags. To avoid confusion, instruct students to wear the name tags for the day.

WRITE YOUR NAME WRITE YOUR NAME WRITE YOUR NAME WRITE

Handprint Name Tags

As a variation to Xeroxes, have the smaller children trace their own handprints on colored construction paper. Cut out, write in information and pin to clothes for the day.

SUB HINT
The name tag projects shown make great mini art, time fillers.

Name

Grade

Age

My name is _____ .

I'm in _____ grade.

Tommy

GA1412

School Bus Name Tag

1. Reproduce school bus name tag on yellow construction paper.
2. Cut out.
3. Use markers to color in tires and chrome.
4. Cut out window panes labelled *Cut out*.
5. Color, cut out and glue bus driver and school children to back side of bus so that they show through the cutout windows.
6. Have each child write in his name and pin to clothing for name tag.

Cut out. Cut out. Cut out. Cut out.

My name is

GA1412

Name Tags

1. Reproduce name tags on white paper.
2. Cut out.
3. Color pictures with bright colored markers.
4. Write in information.
5. Pin to clothing for name tag.

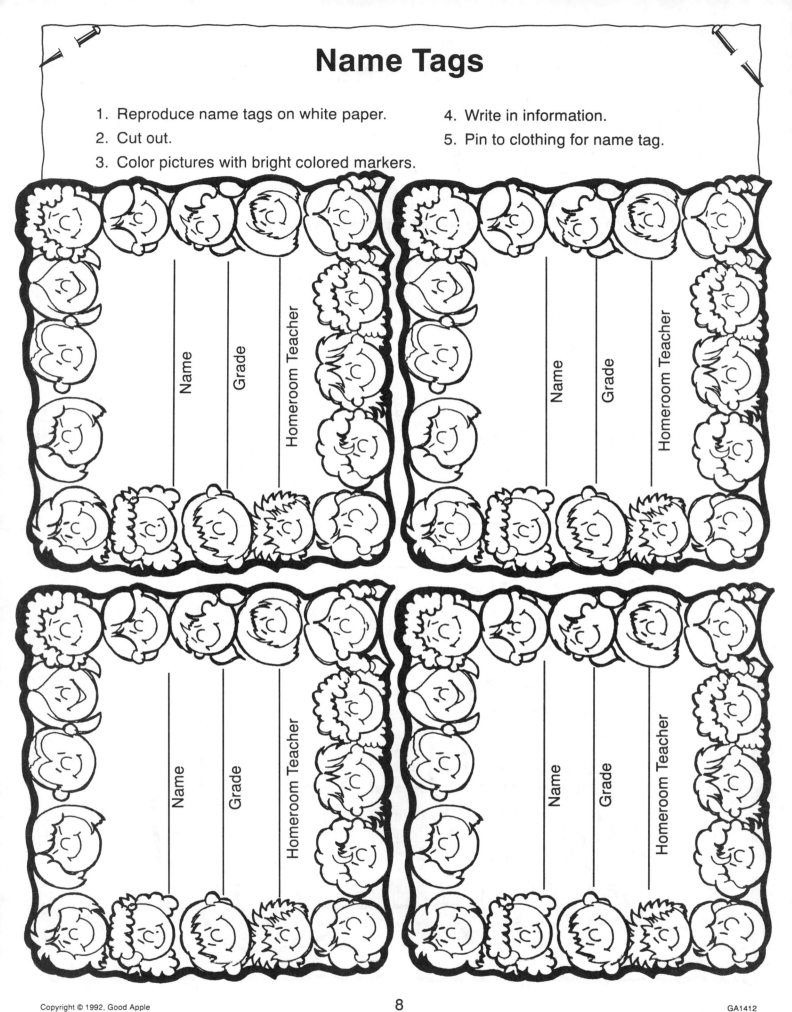

GA1412

Name Tags

1. Reproduce name tags on white paper.
2. Cut out.
3. Color pictures with bright colored markers.
4. Write in information.
5. Pin to clothing for name tag.

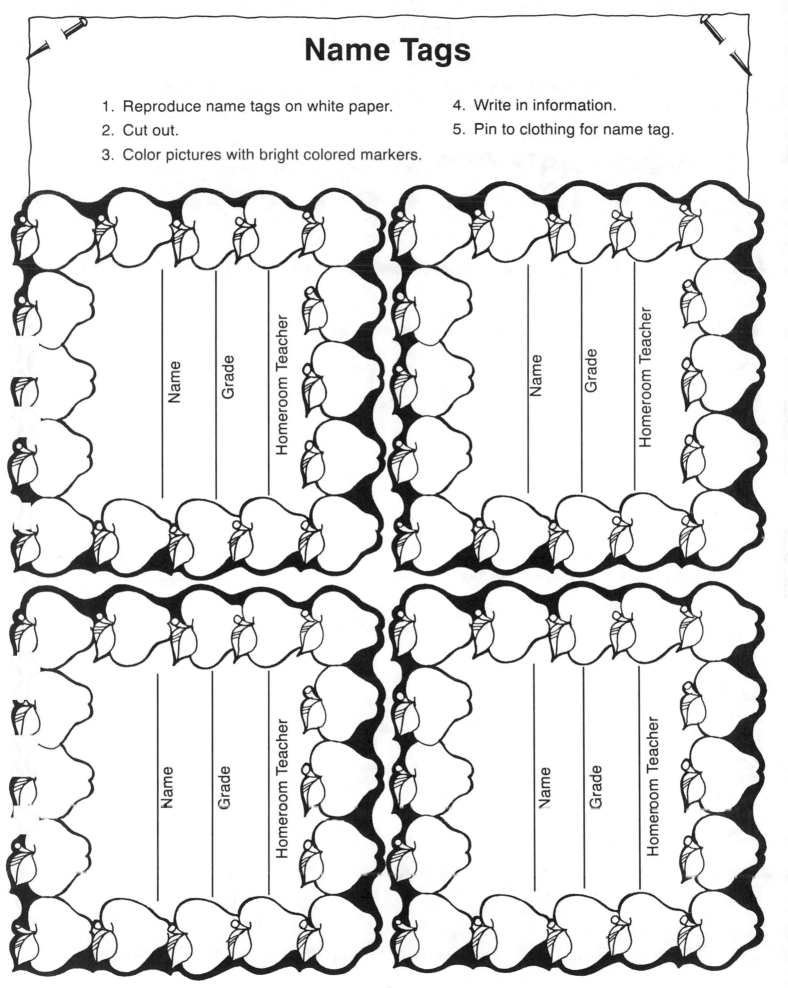

GA1412

Name Tags

1. Reproduce name tags on white paper.
2. Cut out.
3. Color pictures with bright colored markers.
4. Write in information.
5. Pin to clothing for name tag.

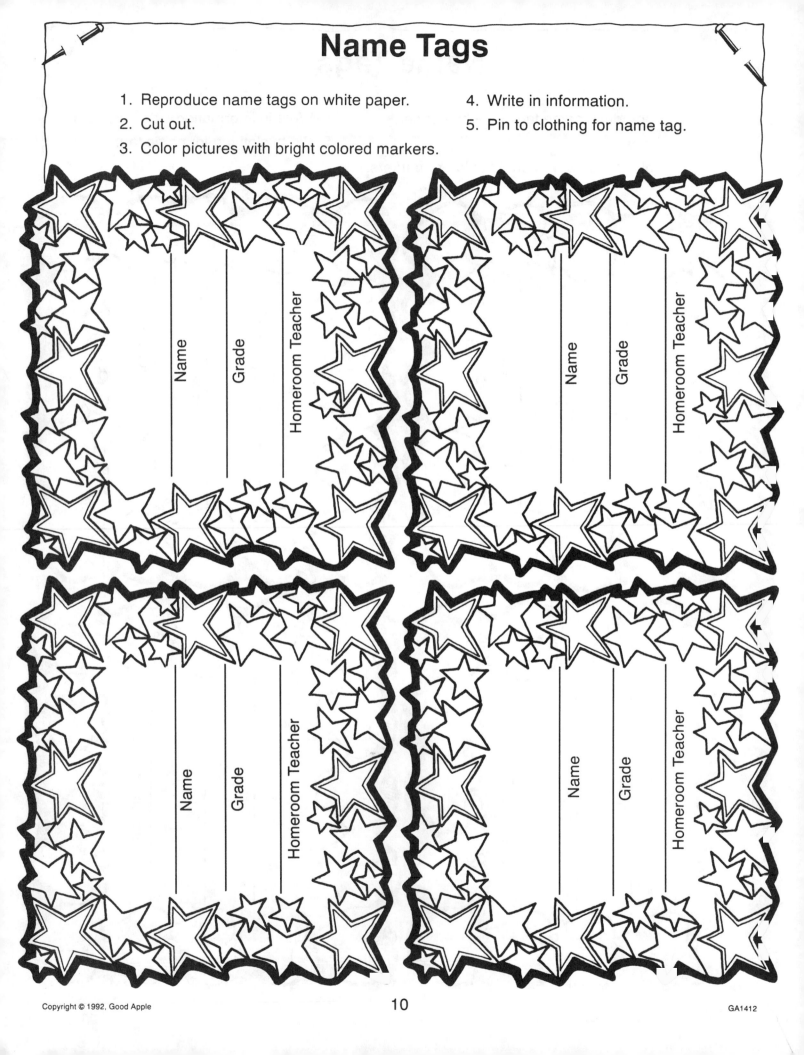

10

GA1412

Name Tags

1. Reproduce name tags on white paper.
2. Cut out.
3. Color pictures with bright colored markers.
4. Write in information.
5. Pin to clothing for name tag.

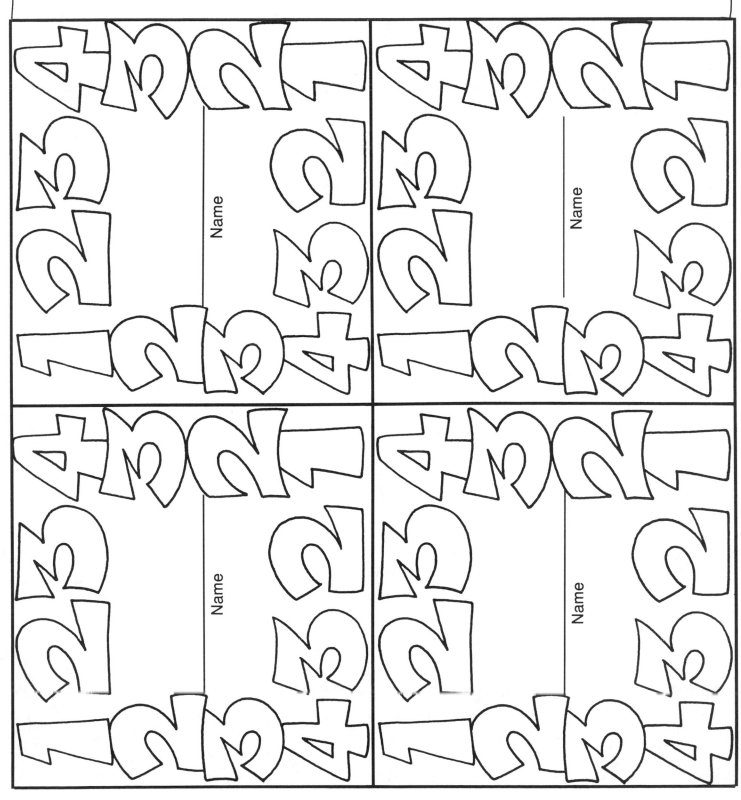

GA1412

Name Tags

1. Reproduce name tags on white paper.
2. Cut out.
3. Color pictures with bright colored markers.
4. Write in information.
5. Pin to clothing for name tag.

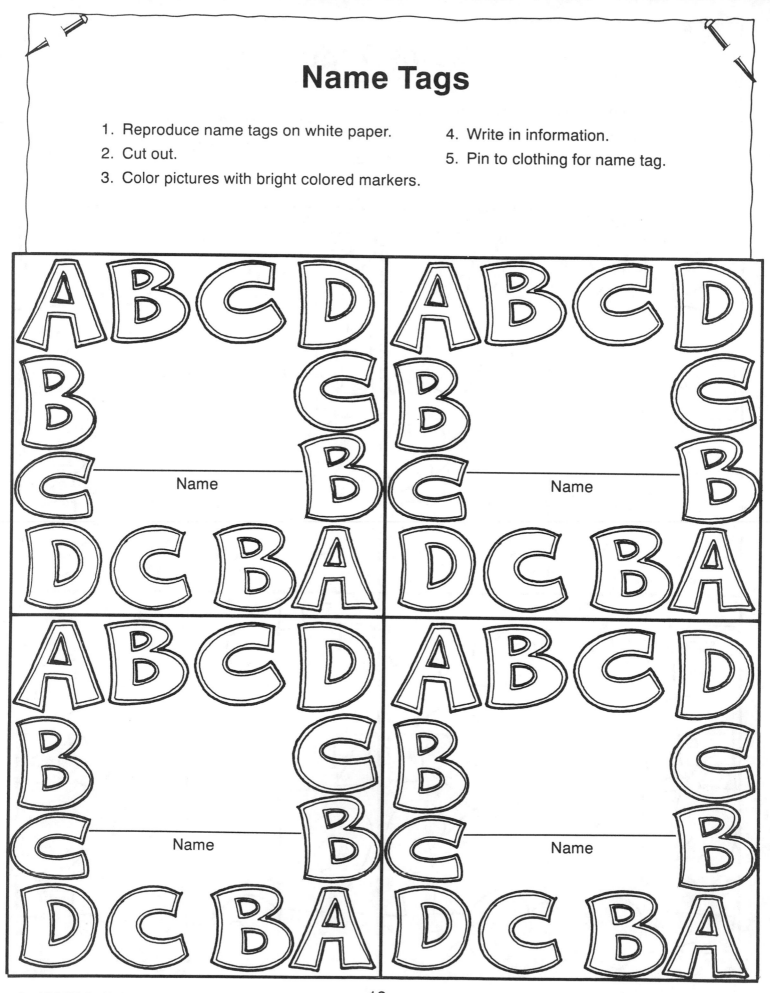

GA1412

Carry Your Own Index Cards

Often a teacher is caught off guard and must be absent unexpectedly. Rarely, but occasionally, a teacher may not be able to leave explicit plans for a substitute.

As a sub you should prepare yourself for that class and any slack time that might occur while you are there. In an attempt to do so, carry your own index card ideas into the classroom with you. You might prepare a set of twenty to thirty index cards on any level or any subject and carry them with you to be used as needed. (However, keep in mind, a good substitute always follows the plans left by the classroom teacher, but a smart substitute is always prepared for anything!)

Several index card ideas follow.

I. Use index cards for penmanship practice.
    A. Write a riddle! Penmanship
       Make up a set of twenty to thirty cards. Write a different riddle on each card. (Write the answer to the riddle upside down near the bottom of the card.)

Write a riddle! Penmanship

Where does a sheep get a haircut?

Answer: At the baa-baa shop.

GA1412

Get your hands on a handwriting book from the school district in which you are substituting. As you write out your cards, follow the guidelines set up in the book to form each letter.

How to use the cards: Give each student one riddle card. Instruct the students to read the riddle, write the riddle according to penmanship guidelines on their own notebook paper and then pass the card on to another student. Continue the process until all students have written all (or part) of the riddles for a penmanship lesson.

Other Riddle Ideas

When are cooks mean?
Answer: When they beat the eggs and whip the cream

How does a dentist examine a crocodile's teeth?
Answer: Very carefully

How do you keep a dog off of the road?
Answer: Put him in a barking lot

What does a puppy say when it sits on sandpaper?
Answer: Ruff

Why does a hummingbird hum?
Answer: Because it doesn't know the words

What do you call a bull when it is sleeping?
Answer: A bulldozer

Why do birds fly South for the winter?
Answer: Because it's too far to walk

What happens to ducks that fly upside down?
Answer: They quack up.

Why do firemen wear red suspenders?
Answer: To hold up their pants

What has four legs but can't walk?
 Answer: A table

What dog keeps the best time?
Answer: A watchdog

When is a farmer mean?
Answer: When he pulls the ears off the corn

GA1412

B. Answer trivia! Penmanship
Make up a set of twenty to thirty cards. Write a different trivia question on each card. (Write the answer to the riddle upside down near the bottom of the card.)

Answer trivia! Penmanship

What is the capital city of the United States?

Answer: Washington, D.C.

How to use the cards: Give each student a trivia card. Instruct students to read the trivia question, write the question and answer according to penmanship guidelines on their own notebook paper. Pass the cards along from one student to another for a penmanship lesson.

GA1412

Other Trivia Questions

Where is the Grand Canyon?
Answer: Arizona

What is a veterinarian?
Answer: An animal doctor

What is hibernation?
Answer: When animals sleep through the winter

What is fog?
Answer: Low clouds

True or False: Your heart is about the size of your fist.
Answer: True

What two colors make the color green?
Answer: Blue and yellow

What is a tortoise?
Answer: A turtle

Who discovered electricity?
Answer: Benjamin Franklin

How many continents are there?
Answer: Seven

Where is Disney World?
 Answer: Orlando, Florida

What does Saturn have that the other planets do not?
Answer: Rings

What is sometimes called "Old Glory"?
Answer: The American flag

How many stars are on the U.S. flag?
Answer: Fifty

What country gave the Statue of Liberty to the U.S.?
Answer: France

Where is the Alamo?
Answer: Texas

What is a foal?
Answer: A baby horse

Who might use a barometer and an anemometer?
Answer: A weatherman

Who wrote *The Adventures of Tom Sawyer*?
Answer: Mark Twain

True or False: Animals that eat meat are carnivorous.
Answer: True

What is the center of the solar system?
Answer: Sun

What is plasma?
Answer: The liquid part of blood

Where would you find the Eiffel Tower?
Answer: Paris, France

What is Braille?
Answer: The alphabet for the blind

For what is a barometer used?
Answer: To measure atmospheric pressure

What is the largest state in the U.S.?
Answer: Alaska

GA1412

C. Dictionary Cards! Penmanship

Make up a set of 26 index cards. Each card should represent one letter of the alphabet. Print 4 words on each card, write their definitions, and draw or paste a small picture to represent each word.

How to use the cards: Pass the dictionary index cards out to your class. Each student should begin with one card. (You may need to make two sets of cards to have enough on hand for larger classes.) Instruct the students to copy the card information on their own notebook paper. Students should follow handwriting guidelines to form each letter and to write each word. (Students should also draw and color their own pictures to represent each word.)

Dictionary Card 1. Penmanship Aa

acorn – a nut

apple – a red fruit

art – a drawing or painting

awake – not asleep

PENMANSHIP

GA1412

When students have completed all twenty-six pages, bind them together with a cover sheet so that each one will have his own dictionary.

Dictionary Card 2. Penmanship Bb

banana - a yellow fruit

bear - a large brown animal

bird - an animal with wings

brown - a dark color

Other Dictionary Word Ideas

#3 Cc
carrot–an orange vegetable
chair–something to sit on
clock–tells time
cook–to make food

#4 Dd
daisy–a flower
draw–to make a picture
duck–a bird that swims
dust–a fine, dry dirt

#5 Ee
ear–what you use to hear
eat–to chew food
elephant–a large animal with a long
    trunk
eye–what you use to see

#6 Ff
farm–where crops are grown
fish–lives in water and swims
float–stay on top of water
friends–good pals

DICTIONARY WORDS • DICTIONARY WORDS • DICTIONARY WORDS • DICTIONARY WORDS • DICTIONARY WORDS • DICTION

GA1412

#7 Gg
game–fun to play
glass–made to hold water and to drink from
green–the color of grass
group–more than two

#8 Hh
hat–covers your head
horse–four-legged animal that you can ride
house–where people live
honeybee–an insect that makes honey

#9 Ii
ice–frozen water
igloo–a house made from snow blocks
ill–sick
insect–very small animal with six legs

#10 Jj
jacket–something worn to keep you warm
jelly–a fruit spread for toast
jump–to leap into the air
jungle–thick with plants and ivies

#11 Kk
kangaroo–animal with pouch that can leap into the air
key–unlocks doors
king–rules over a country
kite–paper object that flies in the wind

#12 Ll
ladder–steps used for climbing
lake–body of water
leg–used for walking
little–small, not big

#13 Mm
mad–not happy, angry
moon–shines on us at night
moose–large four-legged animal with horns
mud–wet dirt

#14 Nn
nap–a short sleep
nest–where a bird lays its eggs
new–not old
numbers–used to count

#15 Oo
oatmeal–warm cereal
open–the opposite of *closed*
orange–the color of a jack-o'-lantern
ostrich–a large bird

#16 Pp
pair–two of anything
panda–a black and white bear
peach–a sweet fruit
pilot–one who flies an airplane

#17 Qq
quack–the sound a duck makes
queen–the wife of a king
quiet–very little noise
quilt–a bed cover

#18 Rr
rabbit–an animal with long ears
red–the color of an apple
rose–a sweet-smelling flower
ruby–a red stone

#19 Ss
sad–not happy
sailboat–boat with sail
seed–from which a plant grows
supper–the evening meal

#20 Tt
table–furniture with legs
toothbrush–used to brush your teeth
tree–very large plant
turtle–animal with a shell

#21 Uu
umbrella–keeps the rain off
uncle–your father or mother's brother
up–not down
usher–one who shows people to their seats

GA1412

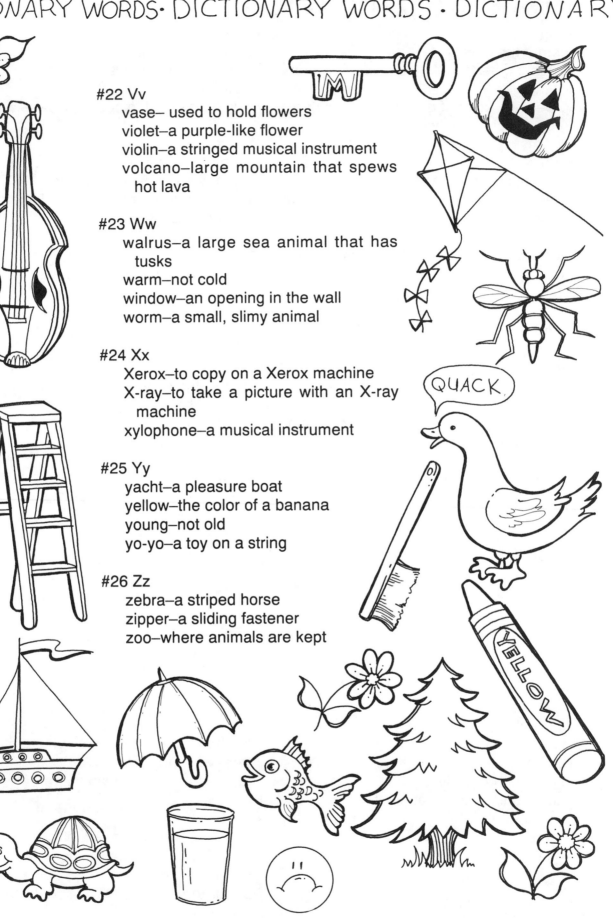

#22 Vv
vase– used to hold flowers
violet–a purple-like flower
violin–a stringed musical instrument
volcano–large mountain that spews
    hot lava

#23 Ww
walrus–a large sea animal that has
    tusks
warm–not cold
window–an opening in the wall
worm–a small, slimy animal

#24 Xx
Xerox–to copy on a Xerox machine
X-ray–to take a picture with an X-ray
    machine
xylophone–a musical instrument

#25 Yy
yacht–a pleasure boat
yellow–the color of a banana
young–not old
yo-yo–a toy on a string

#26 Zz
zebra–a striped horse
zipper–a sliding fastener
zoo–where animals are kept

QUACK

YELLOW

GA1412

II. Use index cards to teach writing.
   A. Use the cards for writing sentences. A *sentence* is a group of words that tells a complete thought.
   There are four kinds of sentences.
   1. A *statement* is a sentence that tells something.
      (A statement ends with a *period*.)
   2. A *question* is a sentence that asks something.
      (A *question* ends with a *question mark*.)
   3. A *command* is a sentence that tells someone to do something.
      (A *command* ends with a *period*.)
   4. An *exclamation* is a sentence that shows strong feeling.
      (An *exclamation* ends with an *exclamation mark*.)

Pretend you are going camping.

Draw a picture of a campsite.

Write five sentences about your camping trip.

1. Write a statement. (Example: I'm going camping.)

2. Write a question.

3. Write a command.

4. Write an exclamation.

5. Write a statement.

Instructions: Make at least five duplicates of each card. Review definitions of different kinds of sentences.

GA1412

Give each student one card and a piece of drawing paper. Instruct students to read the card and follow the directions.

Pretend you are going to the circus.

Draw a picture of the circus.

Write five sentences about the circus.

1. Write a question. (Example: Are you going to the circus?)

2. Write a statement.

3. Write a command.

4. Write an exclamation.

5. Write a statement.

Others

A. Pretend you are having a birthday party. Draw a picture of your birthday party. Write five sentences about your birthday party.
   1. Write a command. (Example: Come to my party.)
   2. Write a statement.
   3. Write a command.
   4. Write an exclamation.
   5. Write a statement.

B. Pretend you are visiting the zoo. Draw a picture of the zoo. Write five sentences about the zoo.
   1. Write a question. (Where are the elephants?)
   2. Write a statement.
   3. Write a command.
   4. Write an exclamation.
   5. Write a statement.

C. Pretend you are in a parade. Draw a picture of your parade. Write five sentences about your parade.
   1. Write an exclamation. (Example: Here comes the parade!)
   2. Write a statement
   3. Write a question.
   4. Write a command.
   5. Write a statement.

D. Pretend you live on a farm. Draw a picture of your farm. Write five sentences about your farm.
   1. Write a statement. (Example: My father is a farmer.)
   2. Write a question.
   3. Write a command.
   4. Write an exclamation.
   5. Write a statement.

GA1412

B. Use the index cards for creative writing.

Make at least five duplicates of each card. Reproduce the pictures, cut out and glue to the index card. Write in the instructions and information with black marker. Give one card to each student in class. Instruct each student to write a story and draw a picture on his own paper.

Students should publish their works by reading their stories out loud to the rest of the class.

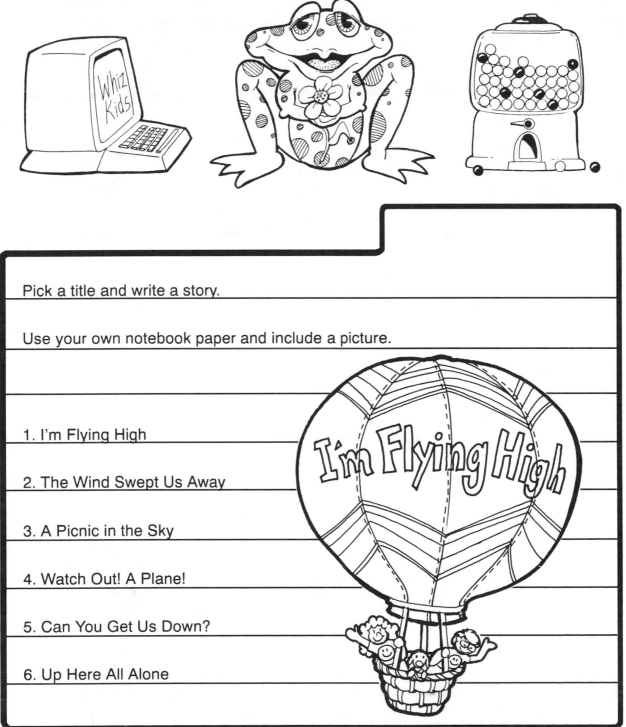

Pick a title and write a story.

Use your own notebook paper and include a picture.

1. I'm Flying High

2. The Wind Swept Us Away

3. A Picnic in the Sky

4. Watch Out! A Plane!

5. Can You Get Us Down?

6. Up Here All Alone

GA1412

Pick a title and write a story.

Use your own notebook paper and include a picture.

1. The Mystery Computer

2. The Computer Whiz Kids

3. Computers Are Fun

4. The Computer Talks

5. The Case of the Missing Computer

6. Who Programmed the Computer?

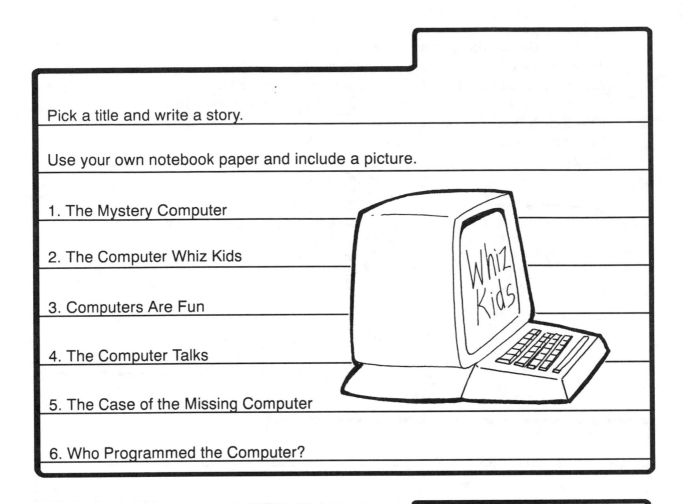

Pick a title and write a story.

Use your own notebook paper and include a picture.

1. The Frog Speaks

2. The Great Green Race

3. Hop Along with Me

4. Frogs in a Pond

5. The Frog in My Pocket

6. The Amazing Mr. Frog

Pick a title and write a story.

Use your own notebook paper and include a picture.

1. Butch Wants the Red One

2. My Very Own Gumball Machine

3. The Empty Gumball Machine

4. Share the Gumballs

5. My Favorite Gumball

6. A Surprise in the Gumball Machine

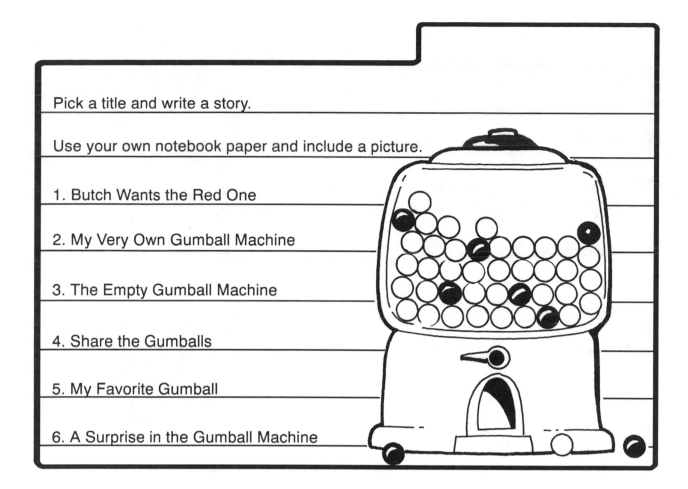

Pick a title and write a story.

Use your own notebook paper and include a picture.

1. Shoot for the Stars

2. Lost in Space

3. On Our Way to Mars

4. Engines Stopped

5. Reentry Mishap

6. The Missing Crew

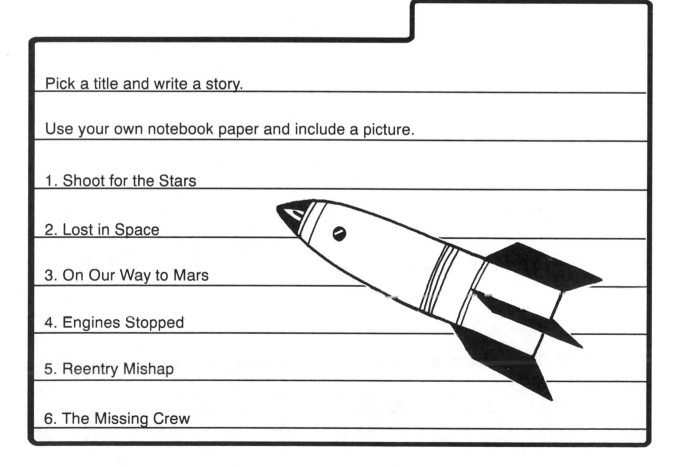

GA1412

Pick a title and write a story.

Use your own notebook paper and include a picture.

1. Chocolate Only

2. Thirty-Nine Flavors

3. Ice-Cream Party

4. Meet Me at the Ice-Cream Parlor

5. Three Dips, Please

6. Ask for Strawberry

Pick a title and write a story.

Use your own notebook paper and include a picture.

1. The Mysterious Mailman

2. Letter to My Pen Pal

3. The Unopened Letter

4. No More Stamps

5. Sounds from the Mailbox

6. My Secret Admirer Writes Again

U.S. Mail

GA1412

Build a Paper City

The following pages provide you with instructions for building a paper city. The only supplies required are scissors, glue, and crayons. The buildings include a house, a grocery store, a bank, a school, a fire station, a hospital, a post office, a police station, and a church.

Reproduce enough instruction sheets for every student in a class to have one. Keep a supply of them in your bag in case you need an emergency activity.

Once the buildings are made, clear an area on a table or on the floor and arrange them so as to represent a city. Once the city is set in place, other activities might be incorporated. Ideas include:

1. Write a story about the paper house you live in.

2. Draw and label a map of the neighborhood.

3. Set up a crime prevention area, and list ideas to prevent crime in your paper neighborhood.

4. Using toy bicycles, set up and demonstrate bicycle safety rules.

5. Write out a recycling of trash program for your paper neighborhood.

6. Divide into groups and plan a treasure hunt for each other throughout the paper neighborhood.

7. Pretend to be a parent. Write out an errand list and a route to follow throughout the paper neighborhood to complete the errands.

8. Label and set up street signs, stop signs, and traffic lights throughout the paper neighborhood.

9. Pick a city block from your paper neighborhood and write a play about the people that live there.

10. Add other items such as parks, lakes, airports, parking lots, railroad tracks, etc., to complete your city.

Build a House

Art

Directions or explanation:

1. Color the house, its family and the dog. Then cut out each piece.
2. Glue the family and dog to the dotted areas that match each form.
3. Cut house and the roof out along the heavy dark lines.
4. Fold on the dotted lines.
5. Glue the dotted area of the house to the inside back fold to form the shape of the house.
6. Glue the dotted areas of the roof to the inside walls to complete the house.

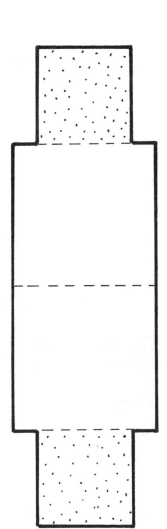

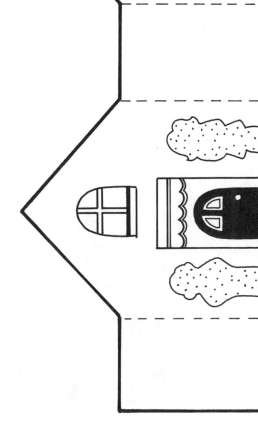

GA1412

Build a Grocery Store

Art

Directions or explanation:

1. Color the grocery store, the grocery men and the grocery carts.
2. Cut out each piece.
3. Glue the grocery men and the grocery carts to the dotted areas that match each form.
4. Color and cut out the roof.
5. Fold on the dotted lines.
6. Glue the dotted area of the grocery store to the inside back fold to form the shape of the store.
7. Glue the dotted areas of the roof to the inside walls to complete the grocery store.

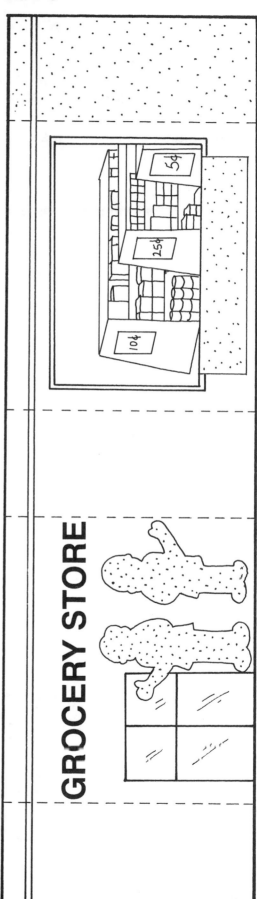

GA1412

Build a Bank

Art

Directions or explanation:

1. Color the bank and the three bank guards.
2. Cut out each piece.
3. Glue the three bank guards to the dotted areas that match the three forms.
4. Color and cut out the roof.
5. Fold on the dotted lines.
6. Glue the dotted area of the bank to the inside back fold to form the shape of the bank.
7. Glue the dotted areas of the roof to the inside walls to complete the bank.

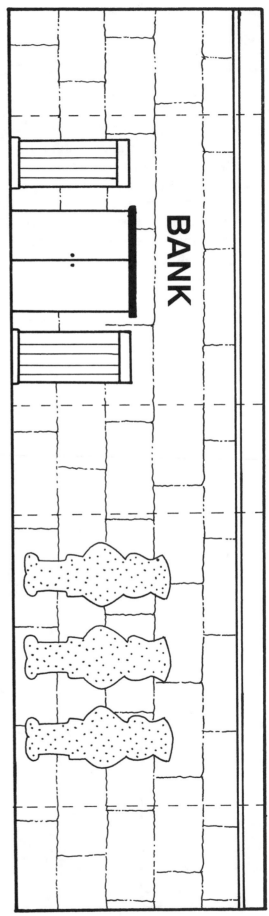

30

Build a School

Art

Directions or explanation:

1. Color the school, the teacher, and the playground scene.
2. Cut out each piece.
3. Glue the teacher and the playground scene to the dotted areas that match each form.
4. Color and cut out the roof.
5. Fold on the dotted lines.
6. Glue the dotted area of the school to the inside back fold to form the shape of the school.
7. Glue the dotted areas of the roof to the inside walls to complete the school.

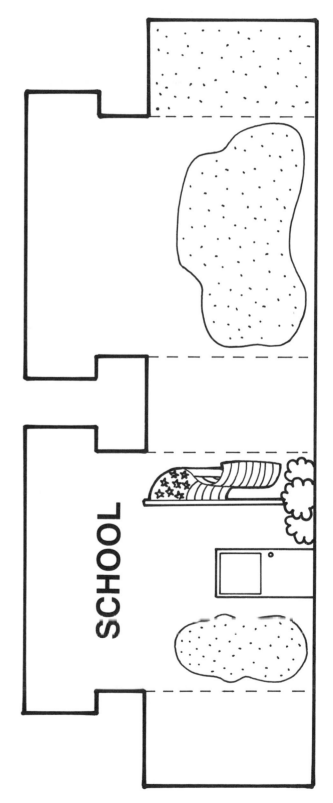

SCHOOL

SCHOOL

GA1412

Build a Fire Station

Art

Directions or explanation:

1. Color the fire station, the fireman, and the fire truck.
2. Cut out each piece.
3. Glue the fireman and the fire truck to the dotted areas that match each form.
4 Color and cut out the roof.
5. Fold on the dotted lines.
6. Glue the dotted area of the fire station to the inside back fold to form the shape of the fire station.
7. Glue the dotted areas of the roof to the inside walls to complete the fire station.

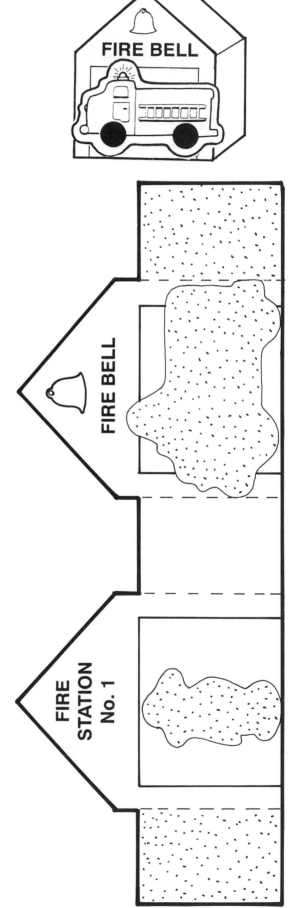

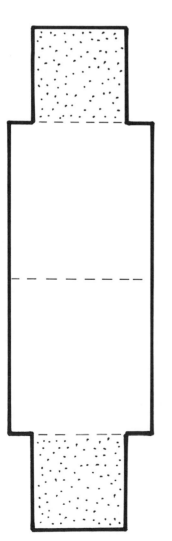

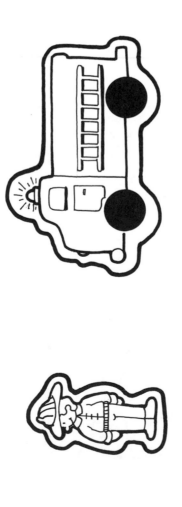

GA1412

Build a Hospital

Art

Directions or explanation:

1. Color the hospital, the Red Cross symbol, and the ambulance.
2. Cut out each piece.
3. Glue the ambulance and the red cross to the dotted areas that match each form.
4. Color and cut out the roof.
5. Fold on the dotted lines.
6. Glue the dotted area of the hospital to the inside back fold to form the shape of the school.
7. Glue the dotted areas of the roof to the inside walls to complete the hospital.

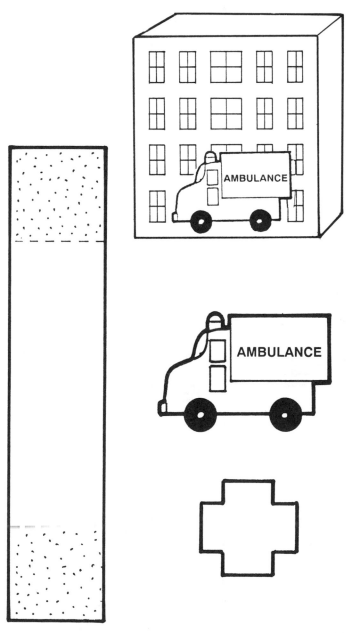

GA1412

Build a Post Office

Art

Directions or explanation:

1. Color the post office, the mailbox, the mail truck, and the flag.
2. Cut out each piece.
3. Glue the mail truck, the mailbox, and the flag to the dotted areas that match each form.
4. Color and cut out the roof.
5. Fold on the dotted lines.
6. Glue the dotted area of the post office to the inside back fold to form the shape of the school.
7. Glue the dotted areas of the roof to the inside walls to complete the school.

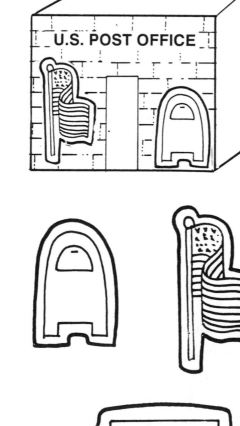

U.S. POST OFFICE

MAIL TRUCK

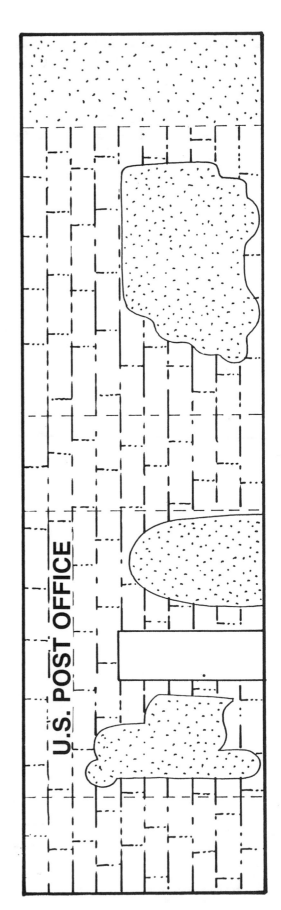

U.S. POST OFFICE

34

GA1412

Build a Police Station

Art

Directions or explanation:

1. Color the police station, the policeman, and the police car.
2. Cut out each piece.
3. Glue the policeman and the police car to the dotted areas that match each form.
4. Color and cut out the roof.
5. Fold on the dotted lines.
6. Glue the dotted area of the police station to the inside back fold to form the shape of the police station.
7. Glue the dotted areas of the roof to the inside walls to complete the police station.

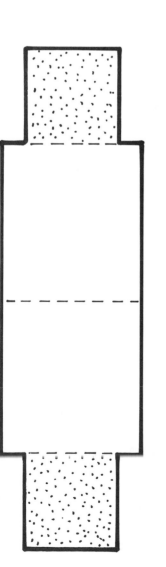

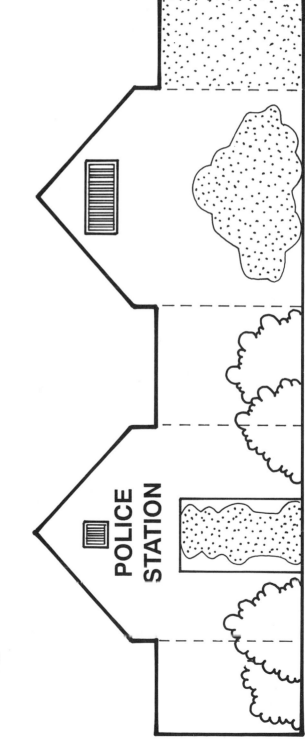

GA1412

Build a Church

Art

Directions or explanation:

1. Color the church, the preacher, the cross, and the stained glass window.
2. Cut out each colored piece.
3. Glue the preacher, the cross, and the stained glass window to the dotted areas that match each form.
4. Color and cut out the roof.
5. Fold on the dotted lines.
6. Glue the dotted area of the church to the inside back fold to form the shape of the school.
7. Glue the dotted areas of the roof to the inside walls to complete the church.

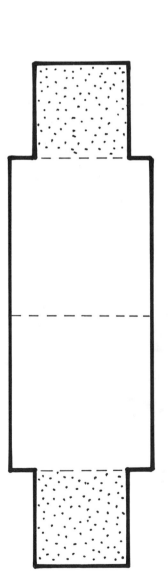

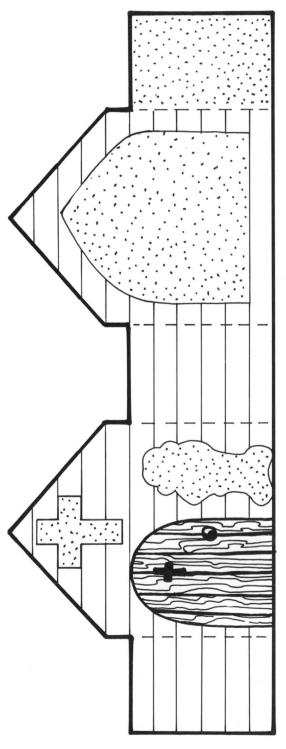

36

Fill in with Math

The math puzzles provided in this book are great learning tools for filling time. As the students work to solve the puzzles, they are able to apply their math skills.

As a substitute, never introduce a new math concept for a classroom teacher unless you are asked to do so. Math can be frustrating to some students, and a substitute teacher does not need frustrated students to deal with. Leave new math material for the classrom teacher to introduce. The students will appreciate her more in this area. They've learned to lean on her in difficulties.

However, math is a great learning tool, and most students love a challenge, so give them math puzzles to solve. Just watch those smiles as they complete the puzzles.

Check the grade level that you will be working in for the day. Run off a set of puzzles or work sheets for that grade and carry them into the classroom with you "just in case."

Give Them Something to Count

Little ones need to learn to count and to write numbers. Reproduce enough of the following paper manipulatives for each child to have a sheet. Have them color, cut out, and glue to the Math Paste Sheet. Count and write the number in the appropriate box.

Math Paste Sheet #1

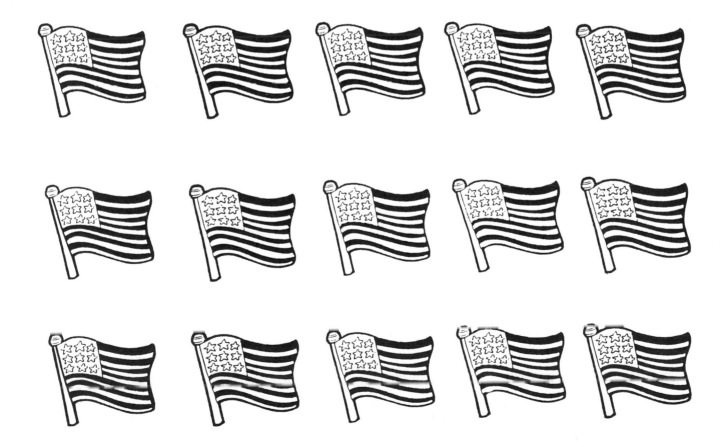

GA1412

Math Paste Sheet #1
1. Count the flag spaces.
2. Paste the appropriate number of flags in the spaces.
3. Trace over the dotted number.
4. Write the number on your own.
5. Write the numbers across the bottom of the page.

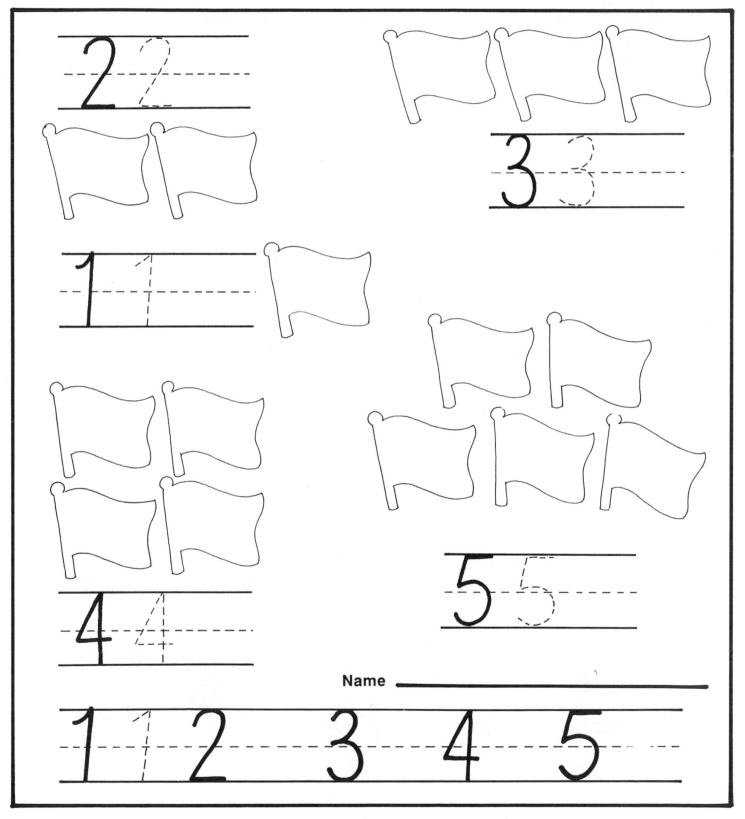

Name _____

38

GA1412

Math Paste Sheet #2

GA1412

Math Paste Sheet #2

Name _____

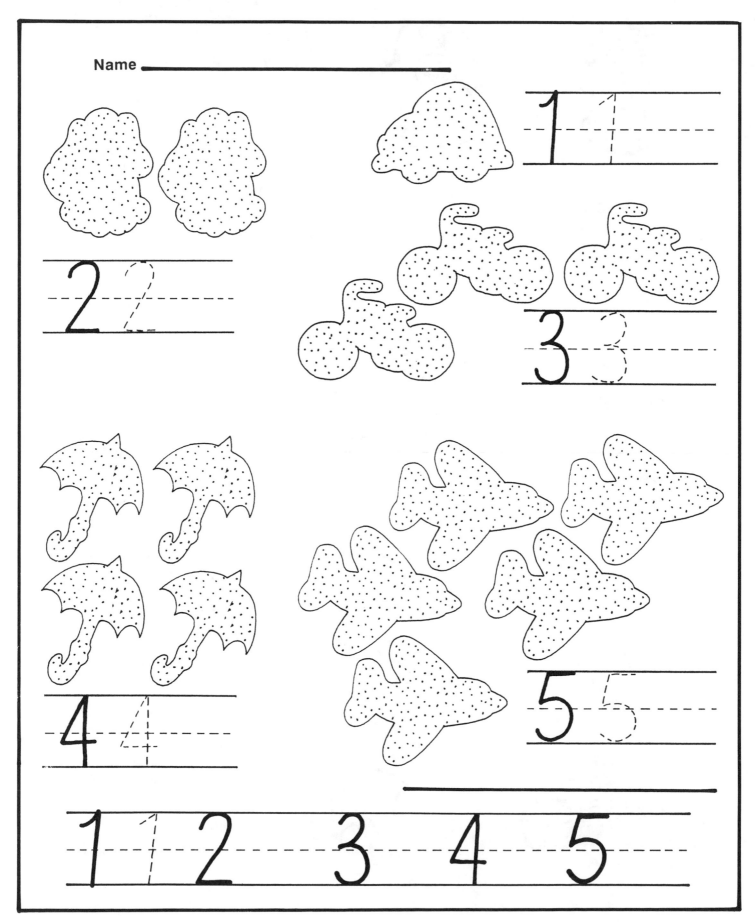

40

GA1412

Math Filler
Read each number sentence and give the sum or ADD.
Read 7 + 2 = 9 as "Seven plus two equal nine."

Find the answer on the teddy bear to the right. Color, cut out, and glue in the correct space.

41

Math Filler
Read each number sentence and give the sum or SUBTRACT.
Read 7 - 4 = 3 as "Seven minus four equals three."

Find the answer on the bunny to the right. Color, cut out, and glue in the correct space.

42

GA1412

Math Fillers

Add to solve the puzzle.

Instructions:

1. Work each problem one at a time.
2. Beginning with the answer to problem number one, draw a line to the answer to problem number two, and so on until the puzzle is complete.
3. Color the picture puzzle, cut out across the dotted line, and turn in with your name filled in the blank.

ADD:

1.	7	2.	8	3.	1	4.	5	5.	2	6.	3	7.	1
	+3		+1		+2		+0		+5		+1		+0
	10												

8.	1	9.	4	10.	3	11.	10	12.	6	13.	9	14.	9
	+1		+4		+3		+9		+6		+6		+9

15.	6	16.	8	17.	10	18.	8	19.	8	20.	9
	+5		+5		+10		+8		+6		+8

Cut here. ---

Name_____

GA1412

Math Fillers
Subtract to solve the puzzle.
Instructions:
1. Work each problem one at a time.
2. Beginning with the answer to problem number one, draw a line to the answer to problem number two, and so one until the puzzle is complete.
3. Color the picture puzzle, cut out across the dotted line, and turn in with your name filled in the blank.

SUBTRACT:

1.	5	2.	6	3.	6	4.	3	5.	10	6.	10	7.	20
	-2		-4		-2		-2		-5		-2		-10
	3												

8.	10	9.	9	10.	8	11.	14	12.	20	13.	30	14.	12
	-1		-3		-1		-2		-1		-10		-1

15.	18	16.	15	17.	19	18.	20	19.	18	20.	20
	-2		-2		-1		-6		-1		-5

Cut here.

- -

Name_____

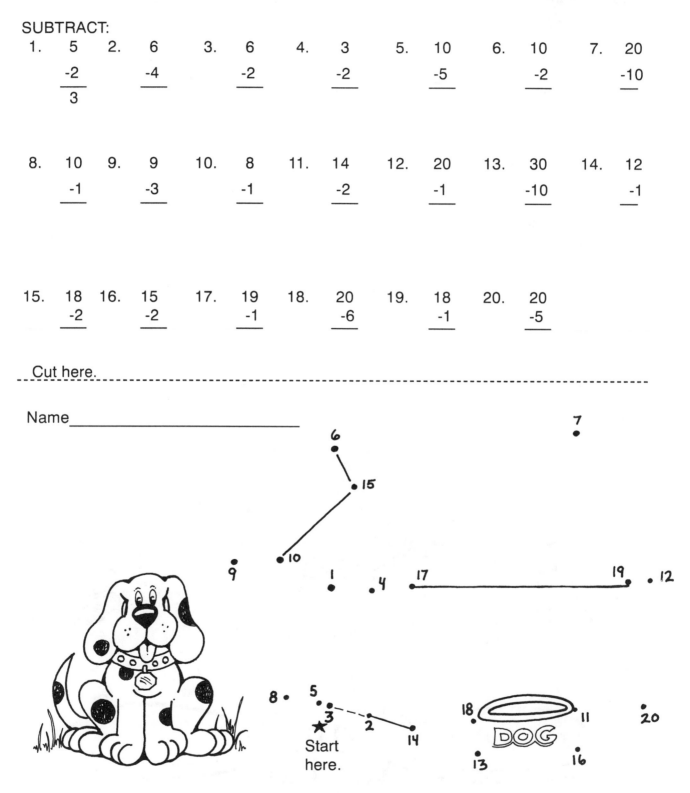

Start here.

GA1412

Math Fillers

Add to solve the puzzle.

Instructions:

1. Work each problem one at a time.
2. Beginning with the answer to problem number one, draw a line to the answer to problem number two, and so one until the puzzle is complete.
3. Color the picture puzzle, cut out across the dotted line, and turn in with your name filled in the blank.

ADD:

1.	73	2.	62	3.	43	4.	50	5.	36	6.	27	7.	39
	+6		+8		+6		+2		+2		+20		+16
	79												

8.	60	9.	38	10.	16	11.	71	12.	56	13.	33	14.	22
	+34		+12		+24		+7		+6		+8		+6

15.	41	16.	67	17.	25	18.	19	19.	44	20.	16
	+5		+28		+38		+20		+37		+11

Cut here.

Name_____

Start here.

27
81•
•79
•70
•49
•52 •55
•38
•47
39
63•
94
78
95
46
41
28
62
•50 •40

GA1412

Math Fillers
Subtract to solve the puzzle.
Instructions:
1. Work each problem one at a time.
2. Beginning with the answer to problem number one, draw a line to the answer to problem number two, and so one until the puzzle is complete.
3. Color the picture puzzle, cut out across the dotted line, and turn in with your name filled in the blank.

SUBTRACT:

1.	42	2.	23	3.	80	4.	68	5.	64	6.	83	7.	34
	-26		-9		-70		-17		-25		-68		-12
	16												

8.	75	9.	73	10.	64	11.	90	12.	59	13.	38	14.	95
	-48		-16		-21		-67		-39		-17		-45

15.	31	16.	86	17.	90	18.	54	19.	40	20.	74
	-24		-75		-35		-48		-10		-29

Cut here.

- -

Name_____

Start here.

★ 16   14
45   10
51 •

50 • 55
20 21 6

30

• 23

• 43
57

39 • • 15
27   22

Copyright © 1992, Good Apple

46

GA1412

Math Fillers

ABC/123 Riddles:

Match the number answer to the letter to solve the riddle.

A B C D E F G H I J K L M N O P Q R S T U V W X Y Z
1 2 3 4 5 6 7 8 9 10 11 12 13 14 15 16 17 18 19 20 21 22 23 24 25 26

RIDDLE: What bus crossed the ocean blue?

MULTIPLY:

1. 3
   x1
   ―
    3

2. 5
   x3
   ―

3. 6
   x2
   ―

4. 7
   x3
   ―

5. 13
   x1
   ―

6. 2
   x1
   ―

7. 3
   x7
   ―

8. 19
   x1
   ―

Answer:

C

Answer: Columbus

47

GA1412

Math Fillers

ABC/123 Riddles:

Match the number answer to the letter to solve the riddle.

A B C D E F G H I J K L M N O P Q R S T U V W X Y Z
1 2 3 4 5 6 7 8 9 10 11 12 13 14 15 16 17 18 19 20 21 22 23 24 25 26

RIDDLE: What is the tallest building in your city?

MULTIPLY:

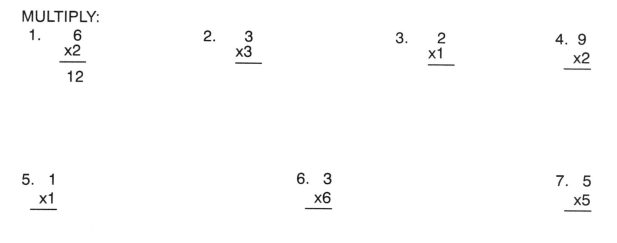

1. 6
   x2
   ___
   12

2. 3
   x3
   ___

3. 2
   x1
   ___

4. 9
   x2
   ___

5. 1
   x1
   ___

6. 3
   x6
   ___

7. 5
   x5
   ___

L _ _ _ _ _ _ _ _

GA1412

Math Fillers

ABC/123 Riddles:

Match the number answer to the letter to solve the riddle.

A B C D E F G H I J K L M N O P Q R S T U V W X Y Z
1 2 3 4 5 6 7 8 9 10 11 12 13 14 15 16 17 18 19 20 21 22 23 24 25 26

RIDDLE: What kind of beans will not grow in your granny's garden?

DIVIDE:

1.
$$2\overline{)20}$$
with work shown:
```
      10
   2│20
     -2
      0
     -0
      0
```

2. $5\overline{)25}$

3. $2\overline{)24}$

4. $4\overline{)48}$

5. $1\overline{)25}$

6. $9\overline{)18}$

7. $2\overline{)10}$

8. $6\overline{)6}$

9. $3\overline{)42}$

10. $2\overline{)38}$

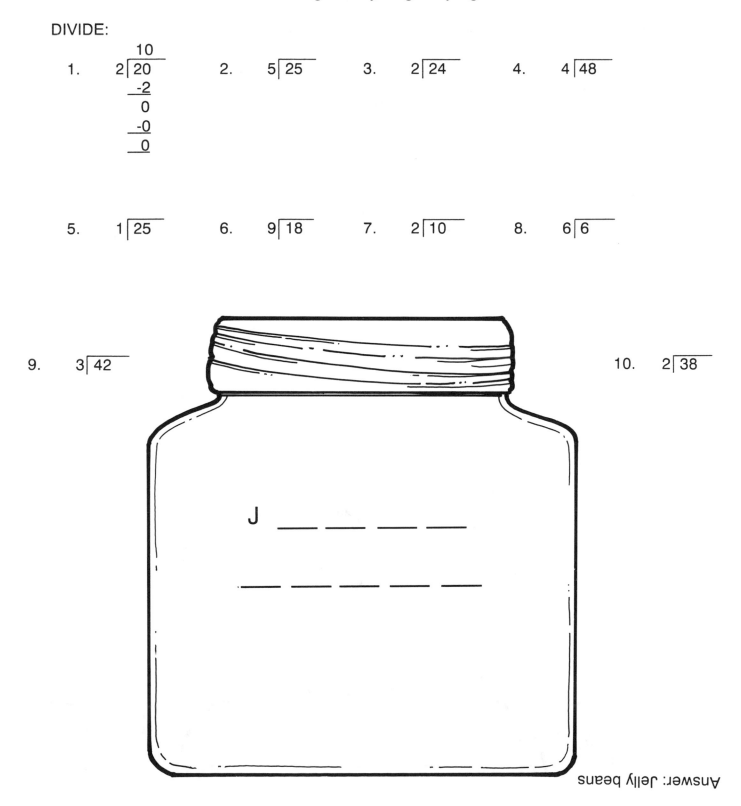

J _ _ _ _ _

_ _ _ _ _

Answer: Jelly beans

49

GA1412

Math Fillers

ABC/123 Riddles:

Match the number answer to the letter to solve the riddle.

A B C D E F G H I J K L M N O P Q R S T U V W X Y Z
1 2 3 4 5 6 7 8 9 10 11 12 13 14 15 16 17 18 19 20 21 22 23 24 25 26

RIDDLE: Why would you want to throw a clock out the window?

DIVIDE:

1.
```
     20
  2 ) 40
    - 4
      0
    - 0
      0
```

2. 2) 30

3. 2) 38

4. 4) 20

5. 5) 25

6. 3) 60

7. 2) 18

8. 3) 39

9. 7) 35

10. 6) 36

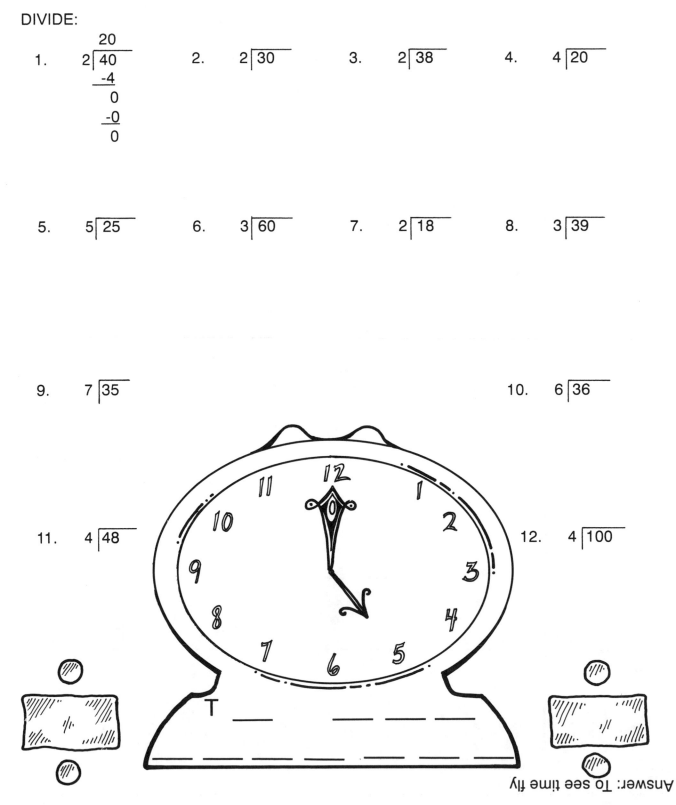

11. 4) 48

12. 4) 100

T ___ ___

GA1412

Color Pop-Up Sheets

Color pop-up sheets can be great fillers for substitute teachers. Choose a pop-up sheet from those provided on the following pages. Reproduce one for each student in the class. (Or, bring a good supply with you into the classroom in which you are substituting for the day.)

Students will need crayons or markers, scissors, and glue to complete the pop-up sheets.

Older students should be encouraged to read and follow the written instructions found on each sheet on their own. Younger children should be guided through the instructions orally as they complete the project.

The pop-up sheets include
>   a seal with a pop-up umbrella,
>   a zebra with a pop-up head,
>   a flag bearer with a pop-up American flag,
>   a sand castle with a pop-up bucket and shovel,
>   a helicopter with front and back pop-up blades,
>   a camping scene with a pop-up tent and a pop-up tree,
>   children with pop-up kites,
>   and baby birds with pop-up eggshells.

Have children color the sheets, cut out the pop-up patterns, and glue them to the sheets according to the directions on each one.

If there is an available space, display the students' work as they complete the pop-up sheets. Children love to have their work exhibited, and their teacher will be pleased to see how hard they have worked in her/his absence.

SUB HINT
Be sure to display everyone's work.

Don't leave anyone out!

GA1412

Color Pop-Up Sheet: Seal

1. Reproduce one sheet and one umbrella part (page 54) for each student.
2. Color sheet and umbrella part.
3. Cut umbrella part out on dark line.
4. Fold up on dash lines.
5. Fold down on dotted lines.
6. Glue outer edges of umbrella part to the dotted areas on sheet to form the pop-up effect.

52

GA1412

Color Pop-Up Sheet: Zebra

1. Reproduce one sheet and one zebra head for each student.
2. Color sheet and zebra head.
3. Cut zebra head out on dark line.
4. Fold on dash lines.
5. With flaps folded under, glue to dotted areas to form the pop-up effect.

Umbrella part:

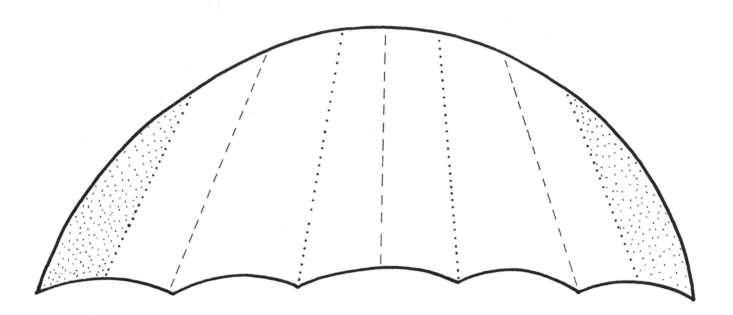

Zebra head:

54

GA1412

Color Pop-Up Sheet: Flag Bearer

1. Reproduce one sheet and one flag (page 57) for each student.
2. Color sheet and flag.
3. Cut flag out on dark line.
4. Fold up on dash lines.
5. Fold down on dotted lines.
6. Match corners and edge to flag outline on sheet and glue to dotted areas to form the pop-up effect.

55

Color Pop-Up Sheet: Sand Castle, Bucket and Shovel

1. Reproduce one sheet and one bucket and shovel (page 57) for each student.
2. Color sheet, bucket and shovel.
3. Cut bucket and shovel out on dark lines.
4. Fold up on dash lines. Match outer edges to bucket outline and glue to form the pop-up effect.
5. Match each end of the shovel to the ends of the shovel outline and glue to form the pop-up effect.

GA1412

Flag:

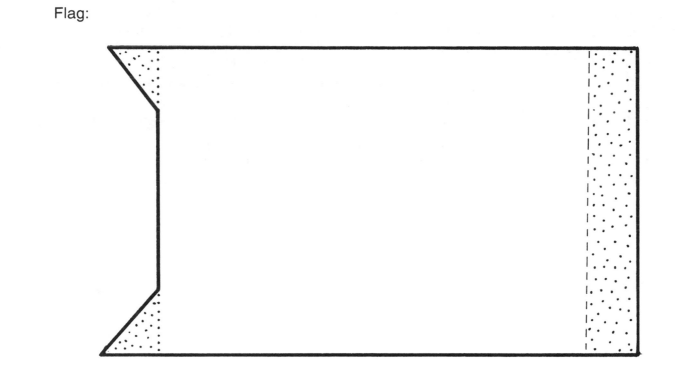

Bucket and shovel:

Color Pop-Up Sheet: Helicopter with Front and Back Blade

1. Reproduce one sheet and one front and back blade (page 60) for each student.
2. Color sheet and blades.
3. Cut blades out on dark lines.
4. Fold front blade up on dash lines. Match center and outer edges of front blade to front blade outline and glue to form the pop-up effect.
5. Fold back blade strip up on dash lines and down on dotted lines to make the accordion-like figure. Glue one dotted end of the accordion-like figure to the back side of the back blade. Glue the other end of the accordion-like figure to the dotted area shown on the back blade outline on the sheet to form the pop-up effect.

GA1412

Color Pop-Up Sheet: Campsite with Tent and Tree

1. Reproduce one sheet and one tent and tree (page 60) for each student.
2. Color sheet and tent and tree.
3. Cut tent and tree out on dark lines.
4. Fold up on dash lines. Match edges of tent to edges on outline and glue to dotted areas to form the pop-up effect.
5. Fold tree on dash line. Match edges of tree to edges on outline and glue to dotted areas to form the pop-up effect.

GA1412

Front and back blades
of helicopter:

Tent and tree:

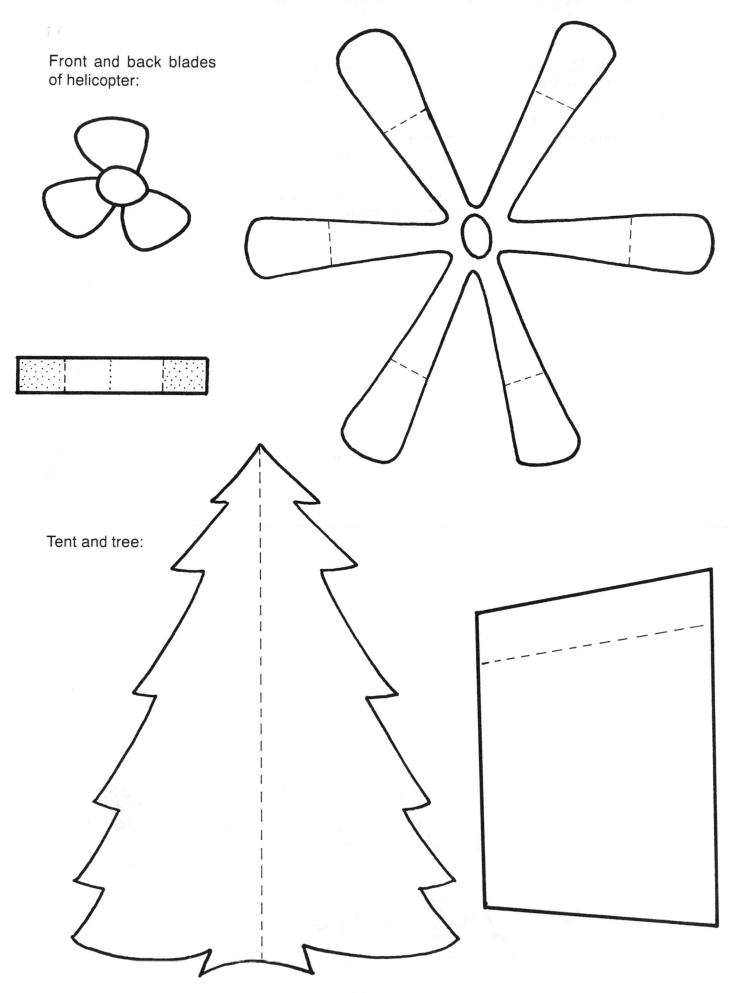

60

Color Pop-Up Sheet: Flying Kites

1. Reproduce one sheet and two kites (page 63) for each student.
2. Color sheet and two kites.
3. Cut the two kites out on the dark line.
4. Fold up on dash lines.
5. Match edges of the two kites to the dotted edges on the outlines and glue to form the pop-up effect.

GA1412

**Color Pop-Up Sheet:
Baby Birds and Eggshells**

1. Reproduce one sheet and the three eggshells (page 63) for each student.
2. Color the sheet and the eggshells.
3. Cut the eggshells out on the dark lines.
4. Fold up on the dash lines.
5. Match the sides and bottom edges of the eggshells to the outlines on the sheet and glue to form the pop-up effect.

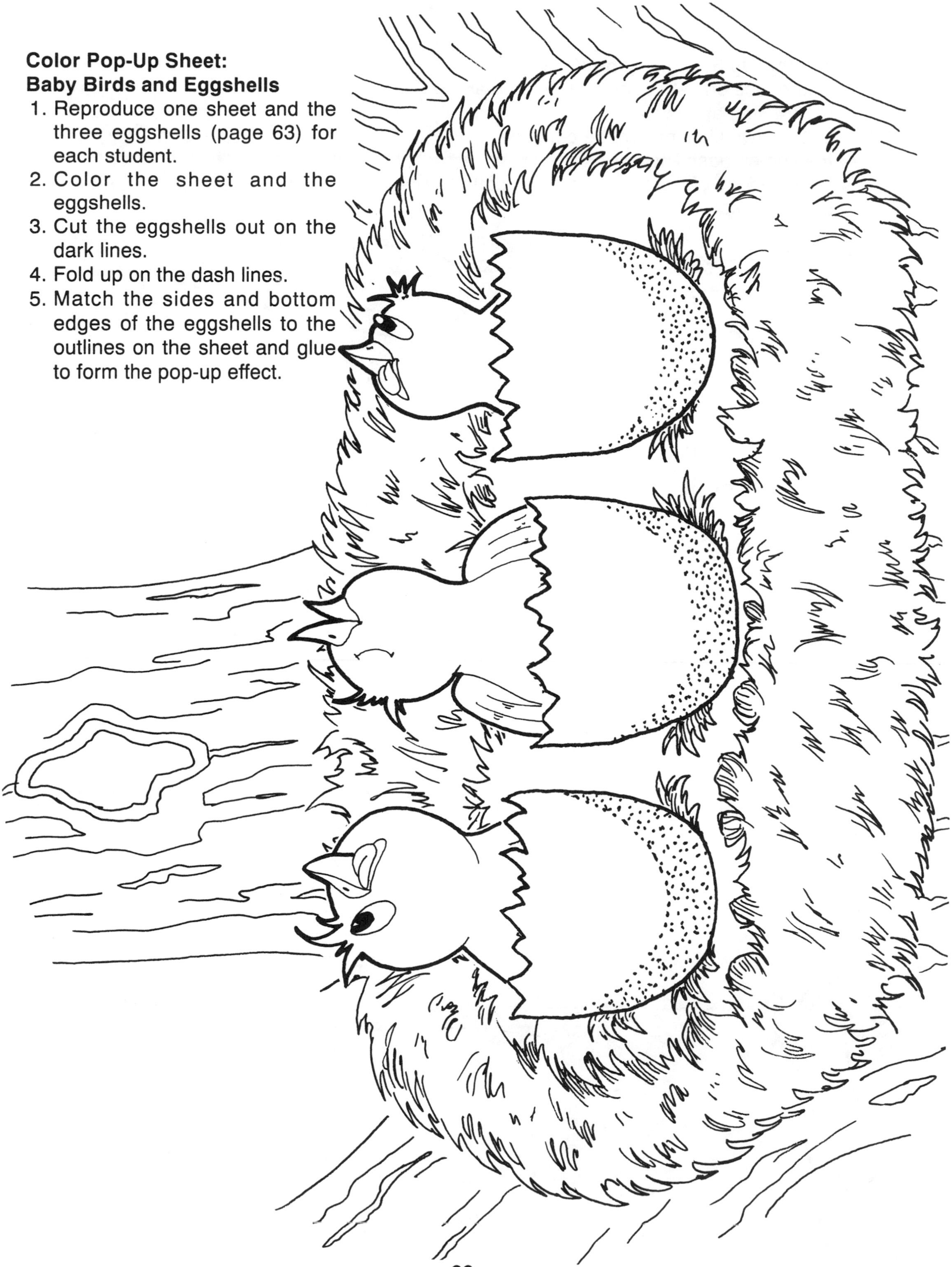

62

GA1412

Two kites:

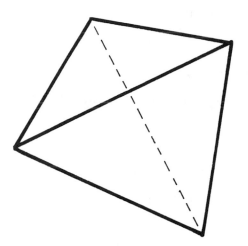

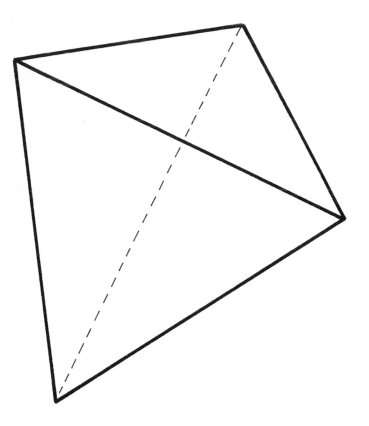

Eggshells:

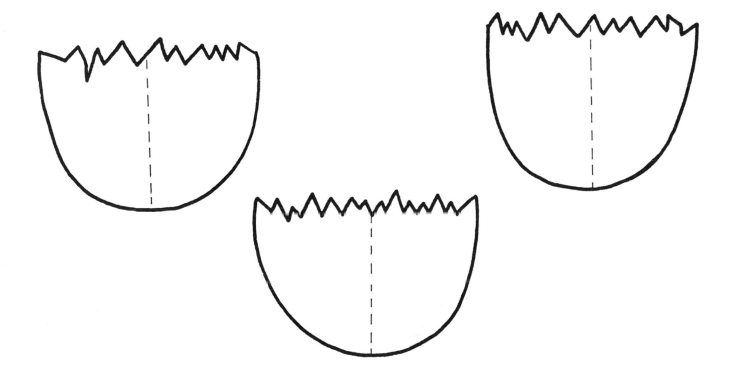

63

GA1412

Map Skills

The map skill sheets found on the following pages were designed to reinforce studies in United States geography. In addition to being great fillers for a substitute teacher, they are wonderful learning tools as well.

Reproduce the map sheets and take a good supply (25 to 35) with you when you accept a substitute teaching job.

Students will need to have access to printed United States maps in the classroom. Have the students research in order to locate and label the information asked for on each sheet.

The map skill sheets include
    the United States plus a state sheet,
    the state of California,
    the state of Colorado,
    the state of Florida,
    the state of Hawaii,
    the state of Idaho,
    the state of Illinois,
    the state of New York,
    and the state of Texas.

Just to get the students warmed up for this activity, ask them the following questions. It might be interesting to see how much they know about the United States geography.

1. In what state would you find Pikes Peak? (Colorado)
2. In what state would you find Everglades National Park? (Florida)
3. In what state would you find the Davis Mountains? (Texas)
4. In what state would you find Pearl Harbor? (Hawaii)
5. In what state would you find Death Valley? (California)
6. In what state would you find the Redwood National Park? (California)
7. In what states would you find Yellowstone National Park? (Wyoming, Idaho and Montana)
8. In what state would you find the city of Chicago? (Illinois)
9. In what state would you find the city of San Antonio? (Texas)
10. In what state would you find Fort Ticonderoga? (New York)

Make up other United States geography questions. Have a contest. See which team of students in the classroom is more skilled in their geography facts about their own country.

GA1412

Name_____

Map Skills: The United States
1. Reproduce one map and one state sheet for each student.
2. Color each state a different color.
3. Cut out each state from the state sheet.
4. Find the location of each state, apply glue, and fit into the correct space.

65

GA1412

Map Skills: California

1. Reproduce one California map for each student.
2. Supply California maps to students. (Examples: wall maps, globes, encyclopedias, etc.)
3. Have students locate and label the following information.

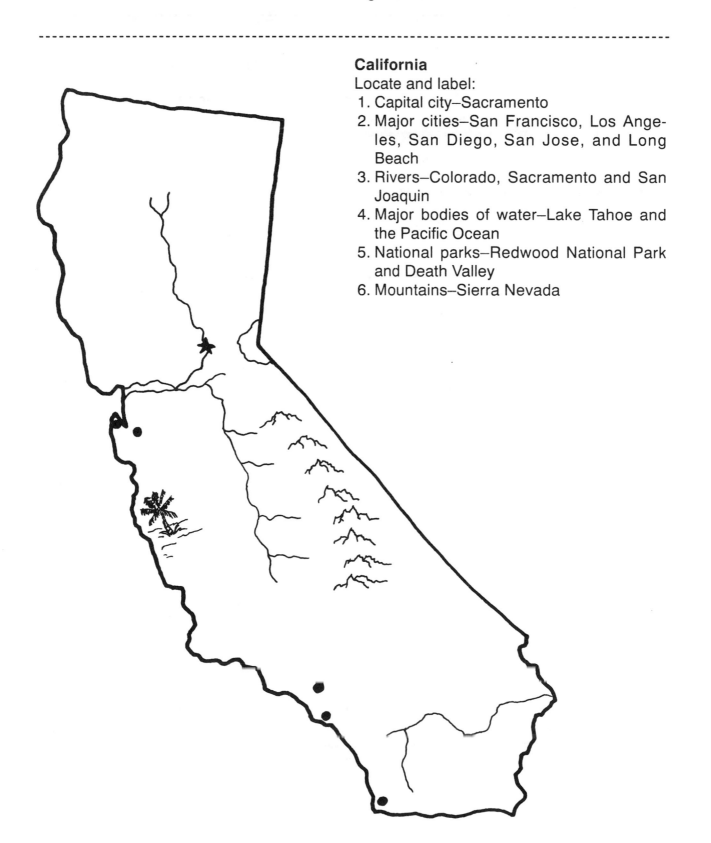

California

Locate and label:

1. Capital city–Sacramento
2. Major cities–San Francisco, Los Angeles, San Diego, San Jose, and Long Beach
3. Rivers–Colorado, Sacramento and San Joaquin
4. Major bodies of water–Lake Tahoe and the Pacific Ocean
5. National parks–Redwood National Park and Death Valley
6. Mountains–Sierra Nevada

GA1412

Map Skills: Colorado
1. Reproduce one Colorado map for each student.
2. Supply Colorado maps to students. (Examples: wall maps, encyclopedias, etc.)
3. Have students locate and label the following information.

- -

Colorado
Locate and label:
1. Capital city—Denver
2. Major cities—Colorado Springs, Pueblo, Fort Collins and Greeley
3. Rivers—Arkansas, South Platte, Colorado and Gunnison
4. Major body of water—Blue Mesa Reservoir
5. National forests—Gunnison, Pikes and Rio Grande
6. Mountains—Rocky Mountains
7. Most famous mountain in the Rockies—Pikes Peak

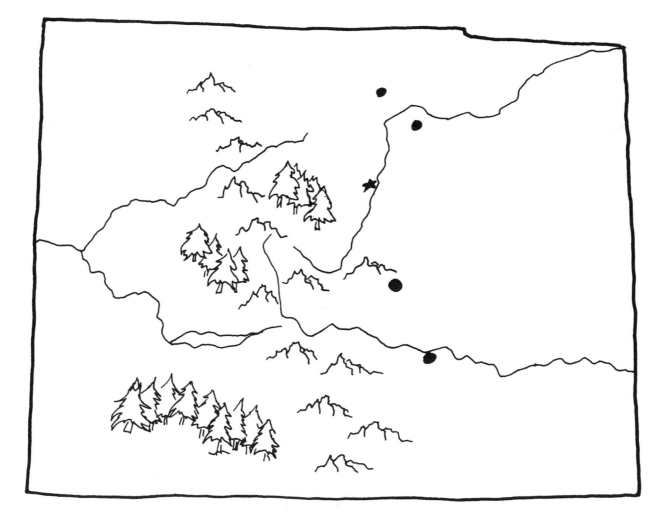

GA1412

Map Skills: Florida

1. Reproduce one Florida map for each student.
2. Supply Florida maps to students. (Examples: wall maps, encyclopedias, etc.)
3. Have students locate and label the following information.

Florida

Locate and label:

1. Capital city–Tallahassee
2. Major cities–Miami, Tampa, Jacksonville, Orlando, Fort Lauderdale and Saint Petersburg
3. Rivers–St. John's, Caloosahatchee, Kissimmee, Peace, Apalachicola and Suwannee
4. Major bodies of water–Lake Okeechobee, Gulf of Mexico and Atlantic Ocean
5. National park–Everglades National Park
6. National forests–Ocala, Apalachicola and Osceola

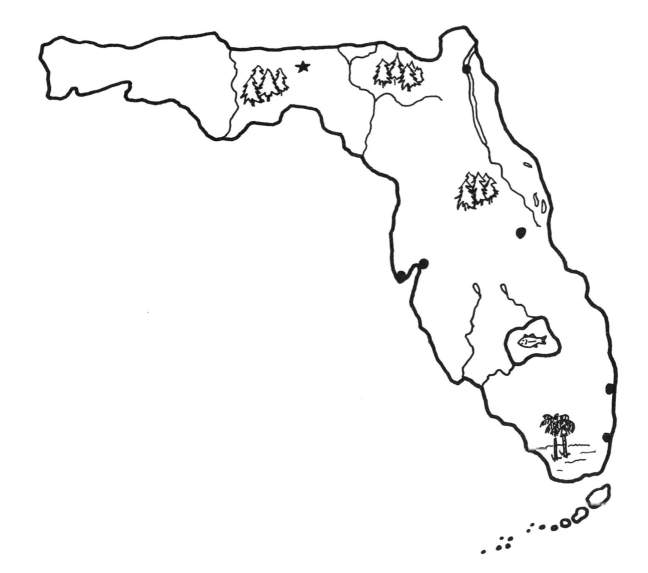

Map Skills: Hawaii
1. Reproduce one Hawaii map for each student.
2. Supply Colorado maps to students. (Examples: wall maps, encyclopedias, etc.)
3. Have students locate and label the following information.

Hawaii

Locate and label:
1. Major islands–Hawaii, Maui, Kahoolawe, Lanai, Molokai, Oahu, Kauai and Niihau
2. Capital city–Honolulu
3. Major cities–Hilo, Wailuku, Kaneohe and Kailua
4. Major bodies of water–Pacific Ocean
5. National parks–Hawaii Volcanoes National Park and Haleakala National Park
6. Historical place of interest–Pearl Harbor
7. Mountains–Koolau Range

GA1412

Map Skills: Idaho

1. Reproduce one Idaho map for each student.
2. Supply Idaho maps to students. (Examples: wall maps, encyclopedias, etc.)
3. Have students locate and label the following information.

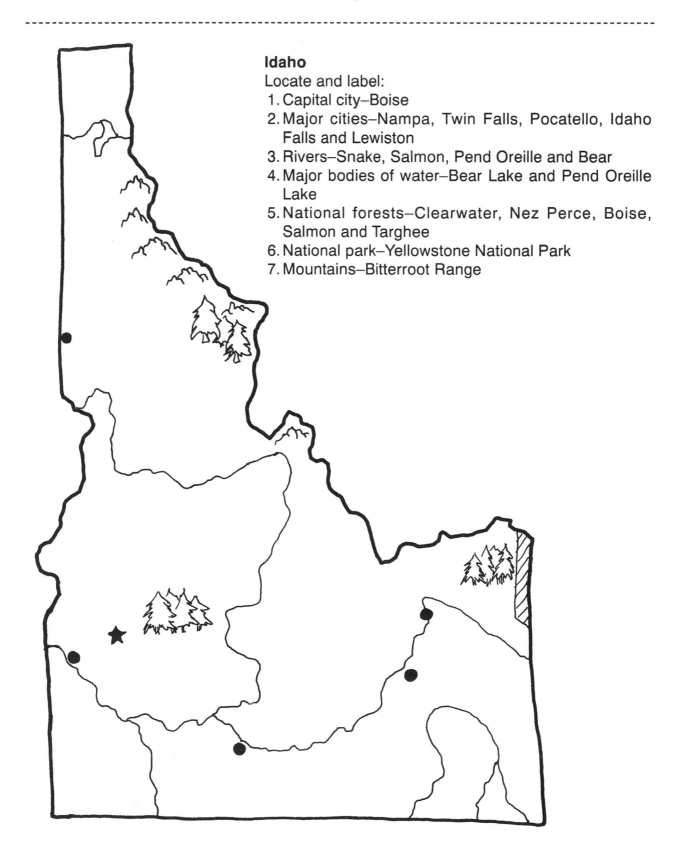

Idaho

Locate and label:
1. Capital city–Boise
2. Major cities–Nampa, Twin Falls, Pocatello, Idaho Falls and Lewiston
3. Rivers–Snake, Salmon, Pend Oreille and Bear
4. Major bodies of water–Bear Lake and Pend Oreille Lake
5. National forests–Clearwater, Nez Perce, Boise, Salmon and Targhee
6. National park–Yellowstone National Park
7. Mountains–Bitterroot Range

71

GA1412

Map Skills: Illinois

1. Reproduce one Illinois map for each student.
2. Supply Illinois maps to students. (Examples: wall maps, encyclopedias, etc.)
3. Have students locate and label the following information.

Illinois

Locate and label:

1. Capital city–Springfield
2. Major cities–Chicago, Rockford, Peoria and Decatur
3. Rivers–Mississippi, Illinois, Rock, Kaskaskia, Ohio and Wabash
4. Major body of water–Lake Michigan
5. National forest–Shawnee National Forest
6. Hills–Quincy Hills and Dubuque Hills

Map Skills: New York
1. Reproduce one New York map for each student.
2. Supply New York maps to students. (Examples: wall maps, encyclopedias, etc.)
3. Have students locate and label the following information.

New York
Locate and label:
1. Capital city–Albany
2. Major cities–New York City, Syracuse, Rochester, Buffalo, Yonkers and Niagara Falls
3. Rivers–Hudson, Mohawk, Genesee, Oswego and St. Lawrence
4. Major bodies of water–Lake Ontario, Lake Erie and Atlantic Ocean
5. Famous forts–Fort Niagara and Fort Ticonderoga
6. Mountains–Appalachian Mountains

GA1412

Map Skills: Texas
1. Reproduce one Texas map for each student.
2. Supply Texas maps to students. (Examples: wall maps, encyclopedias, etc.)
3. Have students locate and label the following information.

Texas
Locate and label:
1. Capital city—Austin
2. Major cities—Dallas, Fort Worth, Houston, San Antonio and El Paso
3. Rivers—Rio Grande, Pecos and Colorado
4. Major body of water—Gulf of Mexico
5. Island—Padre Island
6. National park—Big Bend
7. Mountains—Davis Mountains

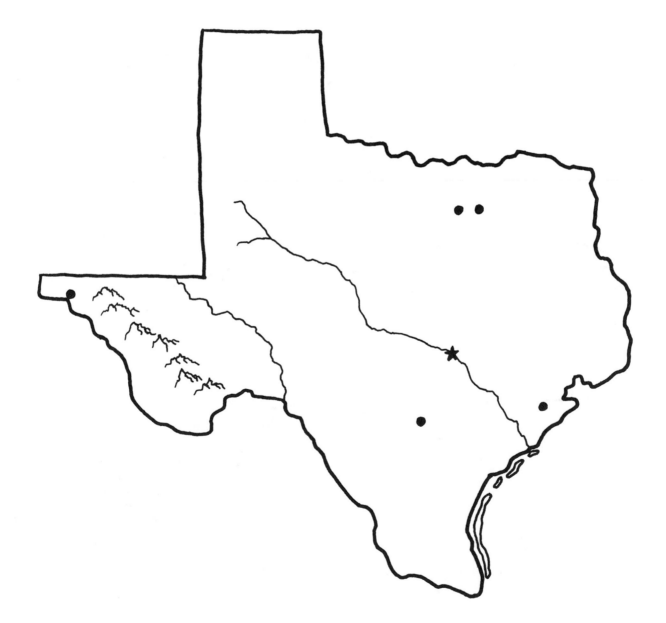

GA1412

Greeting Cards

Use the following greeting cards as mini art projects. Pick out a card depending on the season, or use a teacher card or a friendship card. Have a good supply of runoffs with you when you enter the classroom.

Have the students follow the instructions on each card. Students will need scissors, glue, and crayons or markers for each project.

You will find two teacher cards, two friendship cards, two valentine sheets, a Mother's Day card, a Father's Day card and three Christmas cards from which to choose.

- -

Inside piece for "We Miss Your Smiling Face–Card for Teacher."

GA1412

We Miss Your Smiling Face–Card for Teacher

1. Color front cover of card.
2. Cut out on dark line.
3. Fold on dash line.
4. Color inside piece of smiling face. Cut out on dark line, and glue to inside of card.
5. Send to teacher to say, "Hurry back!"

Dear teacher,
We miss

Apple for Your Teacher—Get Well Card

1. Color inside of card.
2. Cut out on dark lines.
3. Fold on dash line.

4. Color the front cover with bright red and green markers to represent an apple.
5. Send to teacher to say, "We miss you!"

There's a worm in our apple! Get well soon! We miss you!

Dear teacher,

77

GA1412

Friendship Card

1. Draw and color yourself on the front side of figure 1.
2. Draw and color your friend on the back side of figure 2.
3. Color the front side of figure 3.
4. Cut out on dark line.
5. Fold down on the dotted line.
6. Fold up on the dash line.
7. Give to a friend to show how much you like him or her.

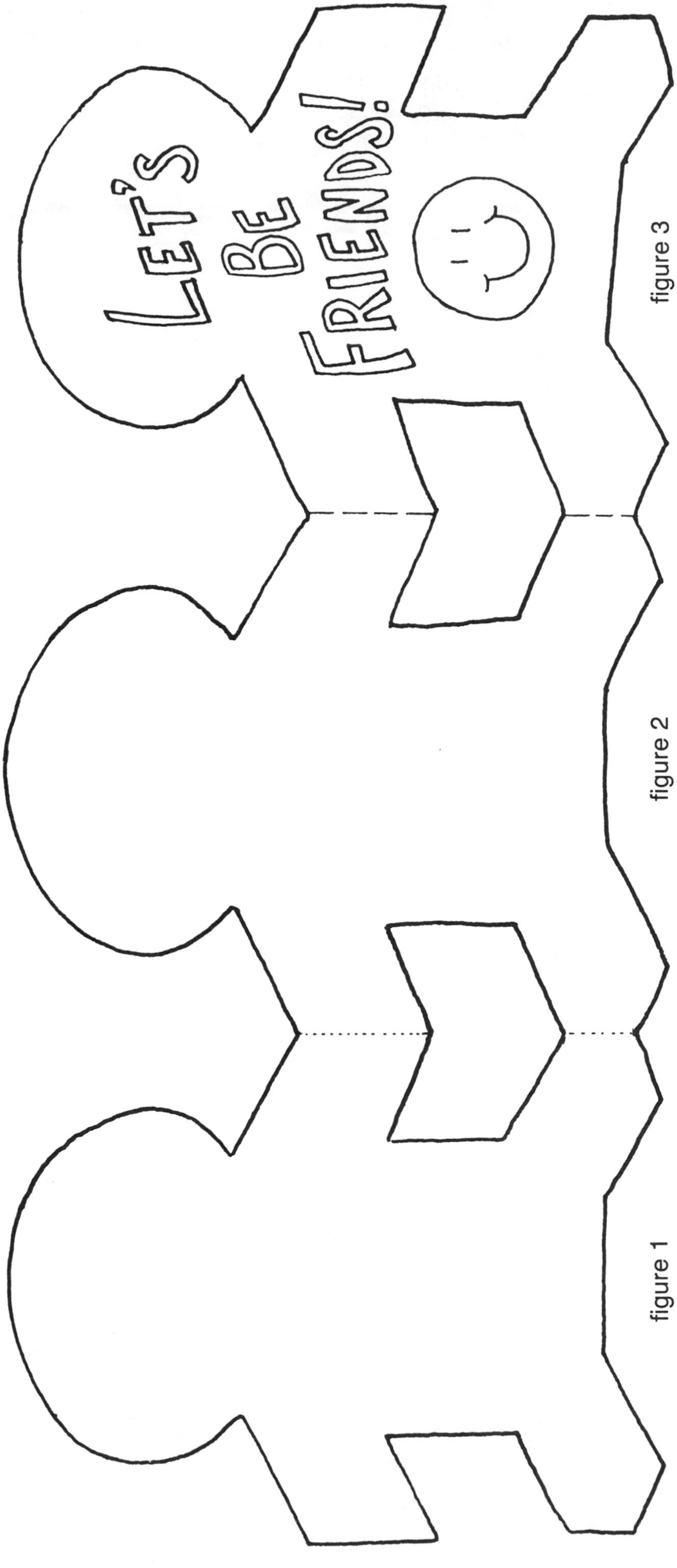

LET'S BE FRIENDS!

figure 3

figure 2

figure 1

GA1412

T-Shirt Friendship Card

1. Color inside letters on card.
2. Cut out on dark line.
3. Fold on the dotted lines to close card.
4. Design and color front cover of T-shirt card.
5. Give to a friend to show how much you like him or her.

So I'm GLAD We're FRIENDS

I'm So GLAD We're FRIENDS

Valentine Cards Color, cut out and give to your valentines.

I break out in spots over you!
Be my valentine!

To:_____

From:_____

Let's seal it! Let's be valentines!

From:_____

To:_____

We'd make a great pair!
Let's be valentines!

To:_____

From:_____

No LION!
You're my valentine!

To:_____

From:_____

80

GA1412

You make
my world
spin around!

Please,
be mine!

To:_____

From:_____

Don't forget!
We're valentines!

To:_____

From:_____

I couldn't BEAR to lose you!
Be my valentine!

To:_____   From:_____

TUSK! TUSK!

I'm all yours!

To:_____   From:_____

GA1412

Mother's Day Card

1. Color card and butterflies.
2. Cut out.
3. Fold on dotted lines along butterfly wings down to make wings stand up.
4. Glue center of butterflies to dotted areas shown in flower centers.
5. Give to your mother on Mother's Day to show honor and love.

Happy Mother's Day

GA1412

Father's Day Card

1. Color card.
2. Cut out.
3. Fold up on dotted lines to form the shape of a man's hat.
4. Write Father's Day message on the inside of the card.
5. Give to your father on Father's Day to show honor and love.

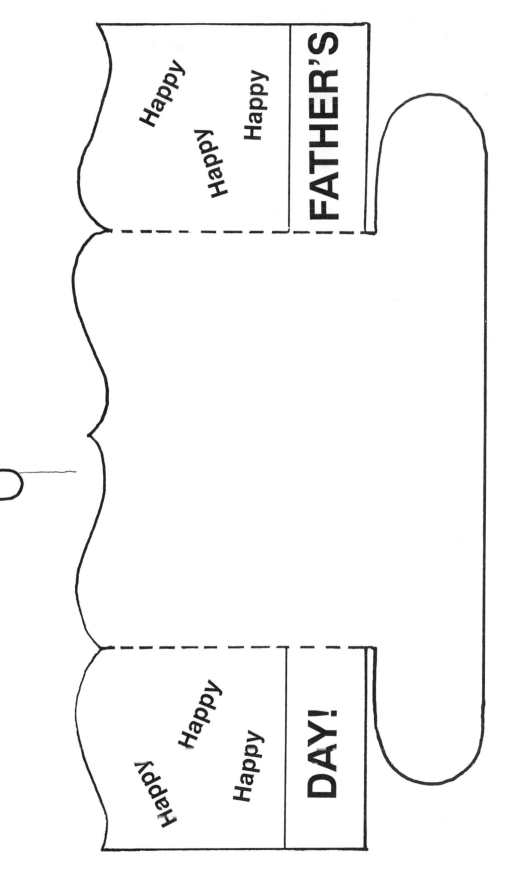

GA1412

Christmas Card Color, cut out and fold on dotted lines to form cards. Write in a

Christmas message and give to a friend.

MERRY ✳ MERRY
MERRY ✳ MERRY

MERRY ✳ MERRY ✳ MERRY ✳
MERRY ✳ MERRY ✳ MERRY ✳ MERRY ✳ MERRY ✳ MERRY ✳ MERRY
MERRY ✳ MERRY ✳ MERRY ✳

GA1412

Christmas Card Color, cut out and fold on dotted lines to form cards. Write in a

HAVE A HAPPY

85

Christmas Card Color, cut out and fold up on dotted lines to form card. Write in a Christmas message and give to a friend.

Ho! Ho! Ho! Ho! Ho! Ho!

86

GA1412

Grab Bag Stories

To prepare the bags:
1. Supply one paper lunch sack per student.
2. Cut out and glue "Instructions for Writing a Story" on one side of sack.
3. Cut out and glue appropriate picture word to the other side.
4. Each sack should include
   a. words to use in writing
   b. blank paper for picture
   c. blank paper for writing story

How to use bags in class:
1. Have each student choose a bag by looking at the word picture on the sack.
2. Instruct students to read the instructions on the side of the sack.
3. Then have them look inside, read the word list, and begin the assignment.

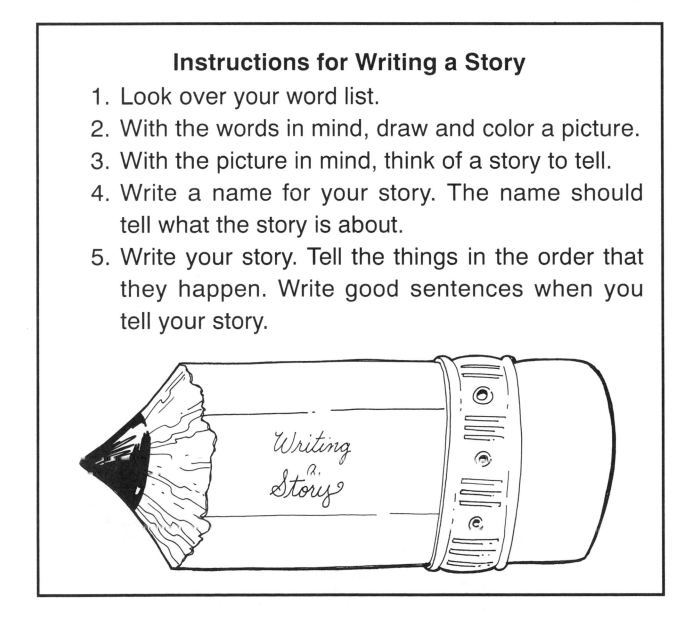

Instructions for Writing a Story

1. Look over your word list.
2. With the words in mind, draw and color a picture.
3. With the picture in mind, think of a story to tell.
4. Write a name for your story. The name should tell what the story is about.
5. Write your story. Tell the things in the order that they happen. Write good sentences when you tell your story.

GA1412

Grab Bag Words

castle	king
knight	queen
dragon	brave
tower	guards
wizard	magic
moat	kingdom

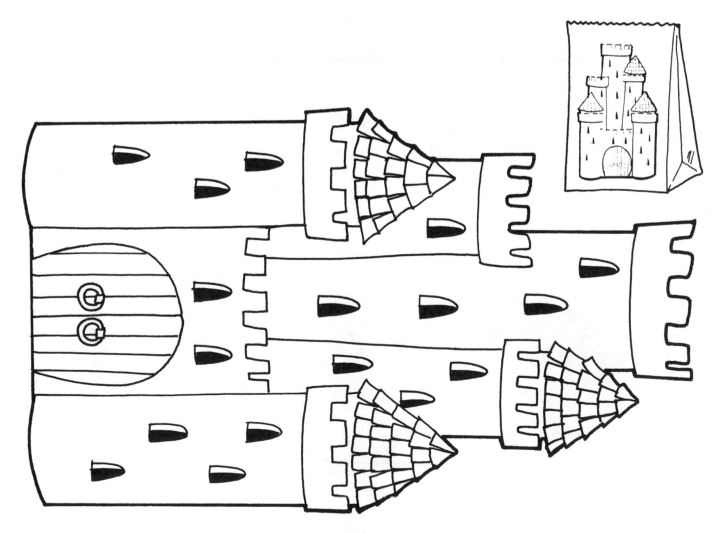

GA1412

Grab Bag Words

space	rocket
stars	comets
astronaut	moon
orbit	controls
earth	aliens
float	gravity

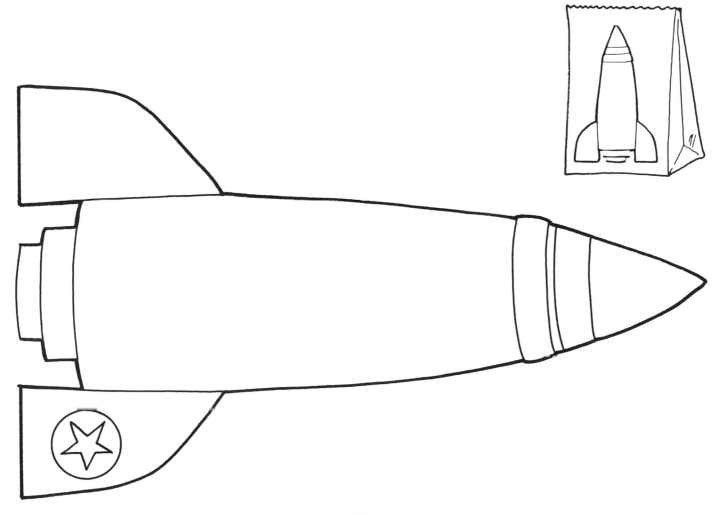

89

GA1412

Grab Bag Words

fireman	fire truck
smoke	house
ladder	hose
water	crowd
hero	cat
climb	trapped

90

Grab Bag Words

haunted	house
ghost	spider
chains	creak
candle	moan
shaking	scared
rattle	scream

GA1412

Grab Bag Words

jungle	elephant
coconut	trees
vines	monkey
tiger	parrot
native	spear
stampede	frightened

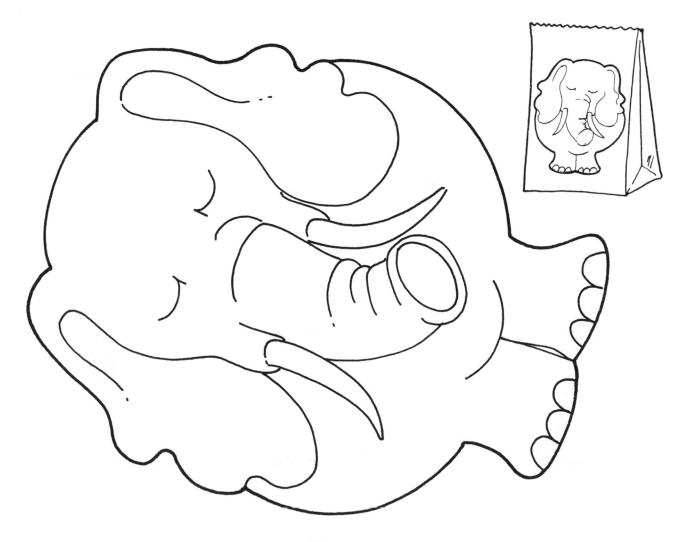

Grab Bag Words

Alaska	Eskimo
sled	dogs
igloo	polar bear
walrus	penguin
seal	iceberg
totem pole	salmon

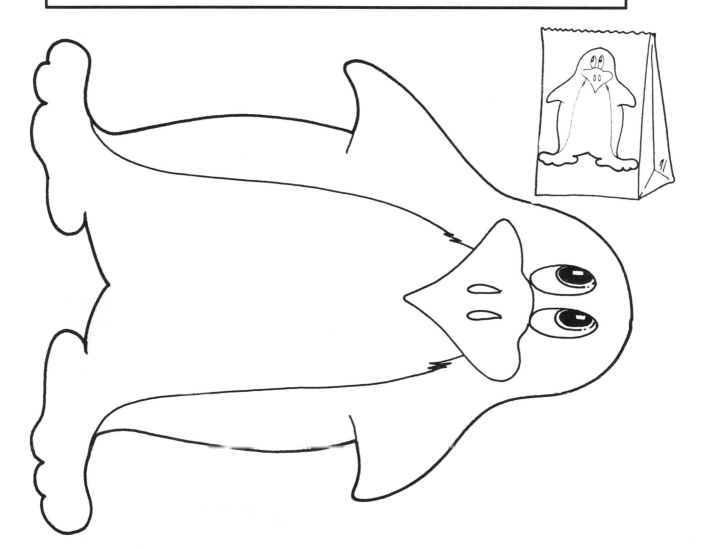

93

GA1412

Grab Bag Words

farm	farmer
pigs	cows
tractor	fence
feed	wagon
barn	hay
pitchfork	sow

GA1412

Grab Bag Words

hospital   accident

doctor   nurse

ambulance   emergency

automobile   parents

police   siren

bandage   stitches

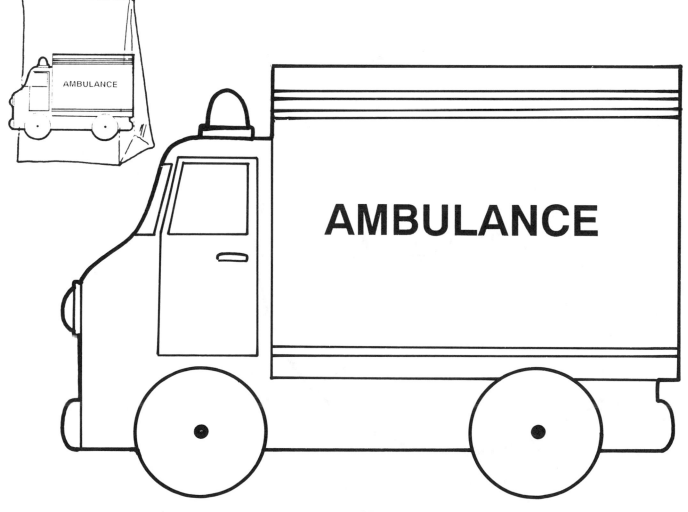

AMBULANCE

GA1412

Grab Bag Words

basketball	win
team	coach
trophy	tournament
dribble	basket
score	lose
cheer	fans

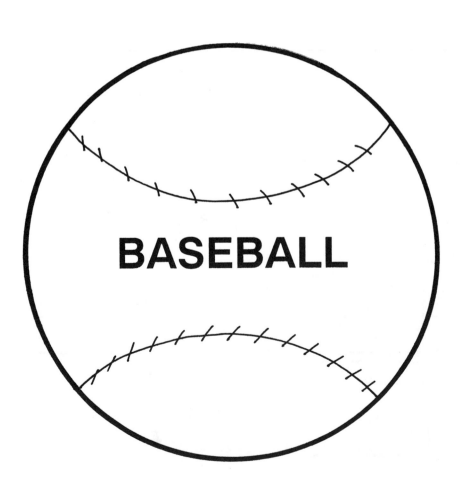

BASEBALL

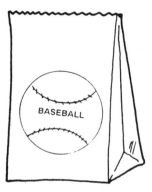

BASEBALL

GA1412

Grab Bag Words

clowns   circus
funny   tricks
makeup   dogs
bicycle   tent
audience   clapped
costume   ringmaster

97

GA1412

Art in General

As a substitute teacher art can be a wonderful experience with the right class. However, some classes need more structured activities with their regular classroom teacher out for the day.

If you happen to be subbing for a class that is mature enough to handle art with a substitute teacher, the following pages offer a few ideas for an exciting art activity.

The art activities include
    three-dimensional shapes
        1. make a cube all about you
        2. make color pyramids
        3. make a rectangular-shaped box

    three-dimensional animals
        1. make a bear
        2. make a lion
        3. make a crocodile

    paper bag puppets
        1. make a clown
        2. make Columbus
        3. make Uncle Sam
        4. make a Thanksgiving turkey
        5. make a snowman

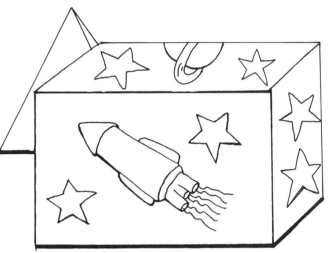

Supplies that the students will need to complete these art projects are simple. The three-dimensional shapes require scissors, crayons, and glue. The three-dimensional animals require scissors, crayons, glue, and construction paper if you choose to use it, and the paper bag puppets require scissors, crayons, glue, and brown paper sandwich bags.

With the exception of the paper sandwich bags, the supplies will most likely be available in the classroom which makes it easy on you, the substitute teacher. However, it is important to always be prepared, so you will want to check with the regular teacher just to be sure.

Art: Make a Cube All About You!

1. Read each block, and write in the answers to the questions.
2. Color and draw in pictures asked for.
3. Cut out on heavy dark line.
4. Fold up on dotted lines.
5. Apply glue to dotted areas, fold cube and glue together.
6. Share with classmates to get to know each other.

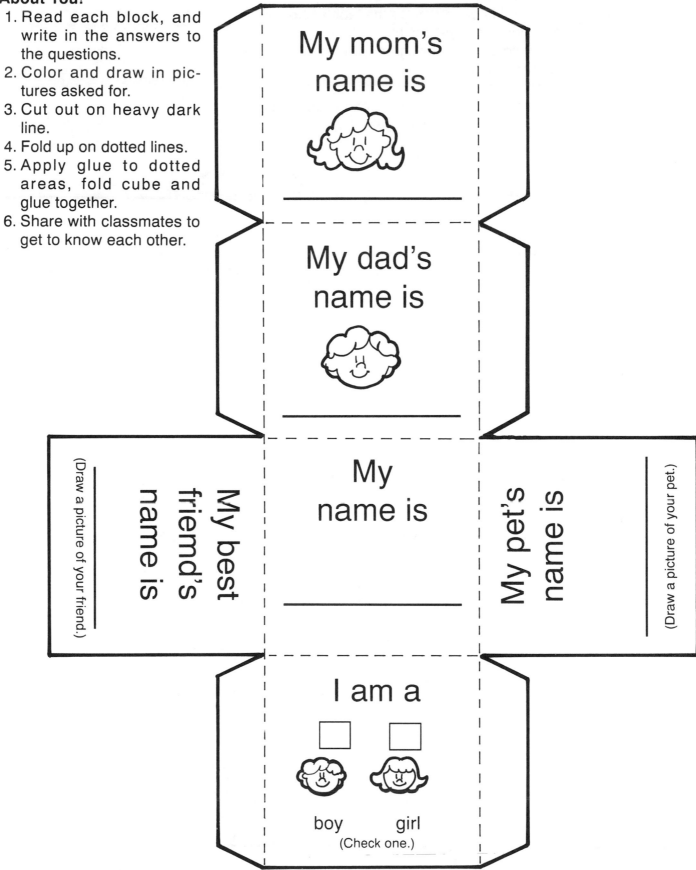

My mom's name is

My dad's name is

My name is

(Draw a picture of your friend.)

My best friend's name is

My pet's name is

(Draw a picture of your pet.)

I am a

boy   girl
(Check one.)

GA1412

Art: Make Color Pyramids

1. Reproduce the two pyramids for each student.
2. Color the pyramids according to the labels shown:
   a. Primary colors—red, yellow, blue
   b. Secondary colors—orange, green, violet
3. Cut out on dark lines.
4. Fold on dash lines.
5. Apply glue to dotted areas. Turn flaps inside, and glue to form the pyramid.

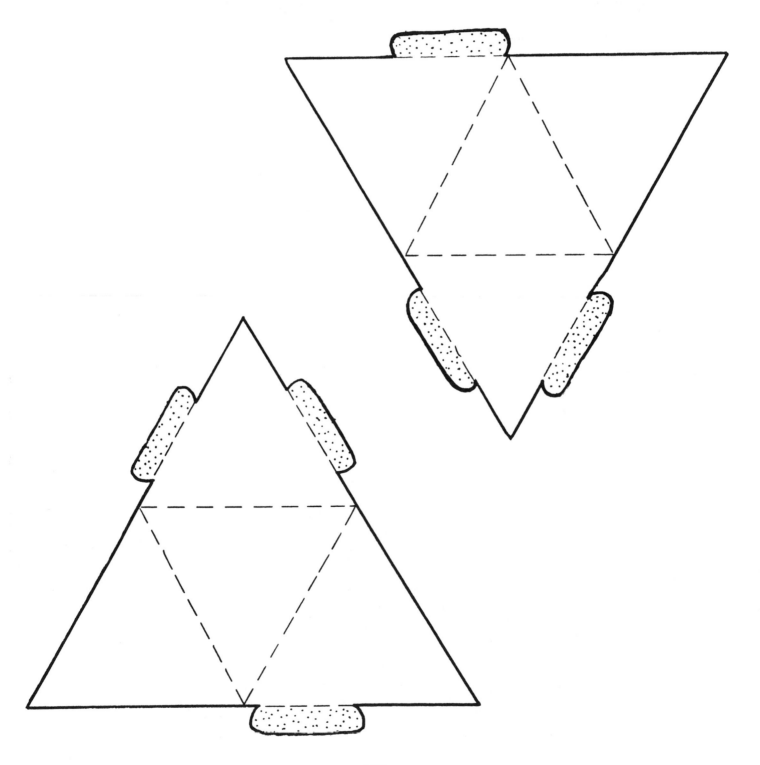

GA1412

Art: Make a Rectangular Shaped Box

1. Color the space scene on the box.
2. Cut out on dark lines.
3. Fold on dash lines.
4. Apply glue to dotted areas on flaps. Tuck inside and glue to form rectangular-shaped box.

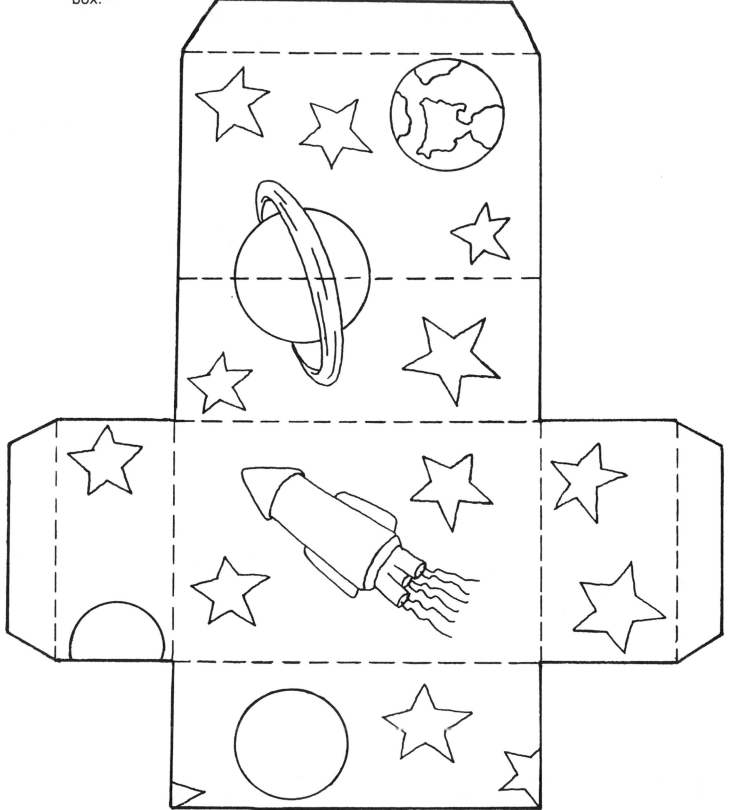

101

GA1412

Art: Make a Bear

1. Color each piece, or cut out of appropriate colored construction paper pieces.
2. Cut out each piece.
3. Fold up on dash lines. Fold down on dotted lines.
4. Glue eyes onto head area in appropriate spaces.
5. Glue teeth to underside of outer edges on top snout.
6. Glue top snout across headpiece onto appropriate dotted area.
7. Glue tongue to top side of bottom snout.
8. Glue bottom snout across headpiece onto appropriate dotted area to complete the bear.

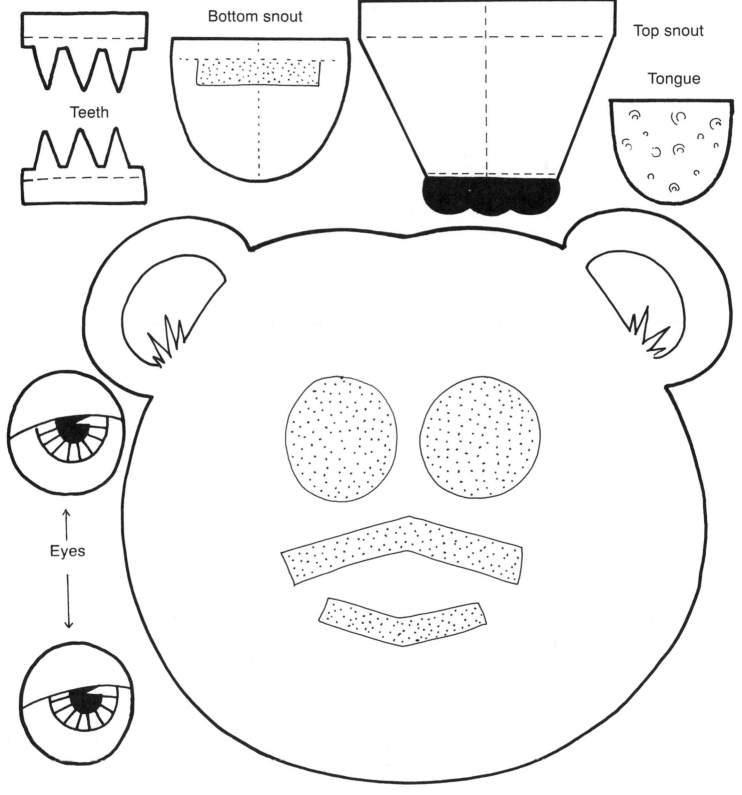

Bottom snout

Top snout

Tongue

Teeth

Eyes

GA1412

Art: Make a Lion

1. Color each piece, or cut out of appropriate colored construction paper pieces.
2. Cut out each piece.
3. See nose. Fold down on dash line. Fold up on dotted line. Apply glue to back side of top flap. Glue onto lion's face to appropriate box.
4. See lion's face. Fold down on dash line. Fold up on dotted lines. Apply glue to each side of cheek areas and glue to appropriate dotted areas of lion's main to form a 3-D effect of the face.

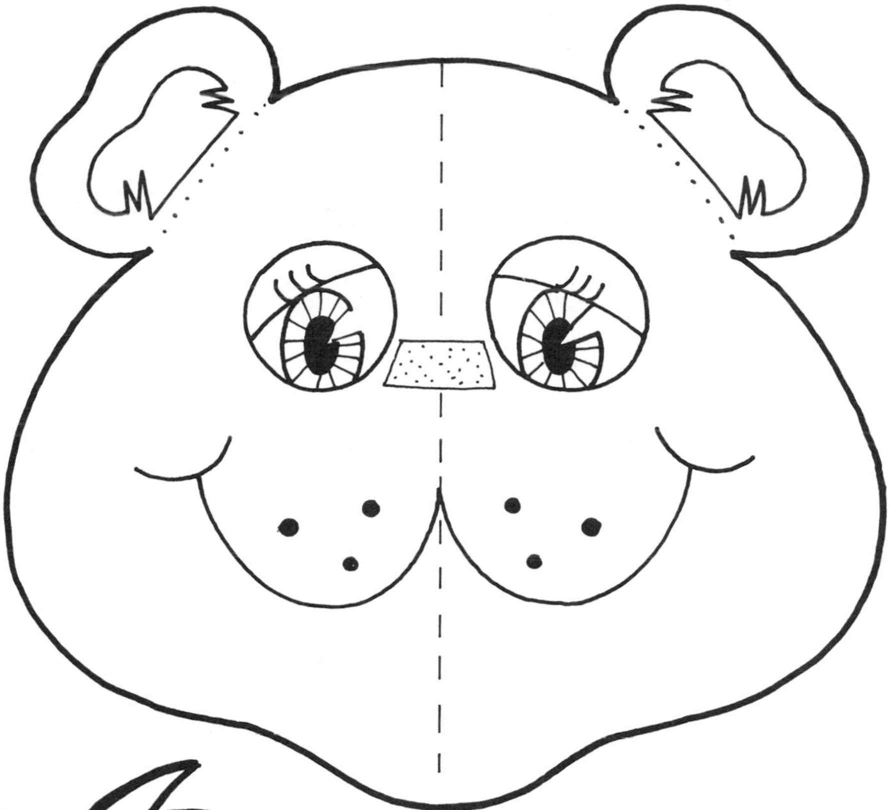

Nose

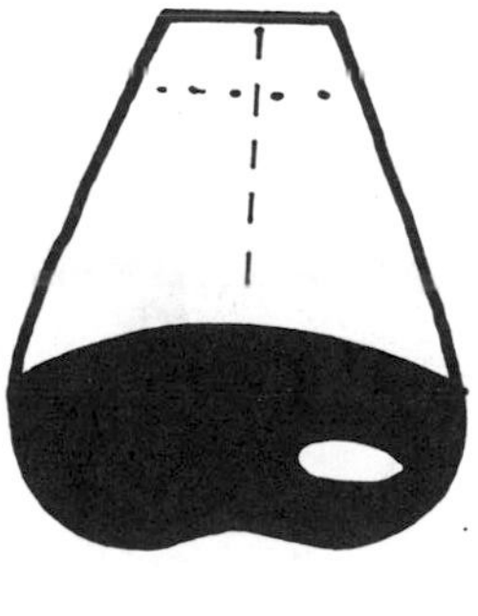

GA1412

Art: Make a Crocodile

1. Color each piece, or cut out of appropriate colored construction paper pieces.

2. Cut out each piece.

3. Fold up on dash lines. Fold down on dotted lines.

4. Glue eyes onto head area in appropriate spaces.

5. Glue top teeth to underside of outer edges of top snout.

6. Glue front fangs to front undersides just below turned up nostrils. Use black construction paper pieces over the areas.

7. Glue top snout across headpiece just under eye area.

8. Glue tongue to top side of bottom snout.

9. Glue bottom teeth to top side outer edges of bottom snout.

10. Glue bottom snout across headpiece just under top snout to complete the crocodile.

GA1412

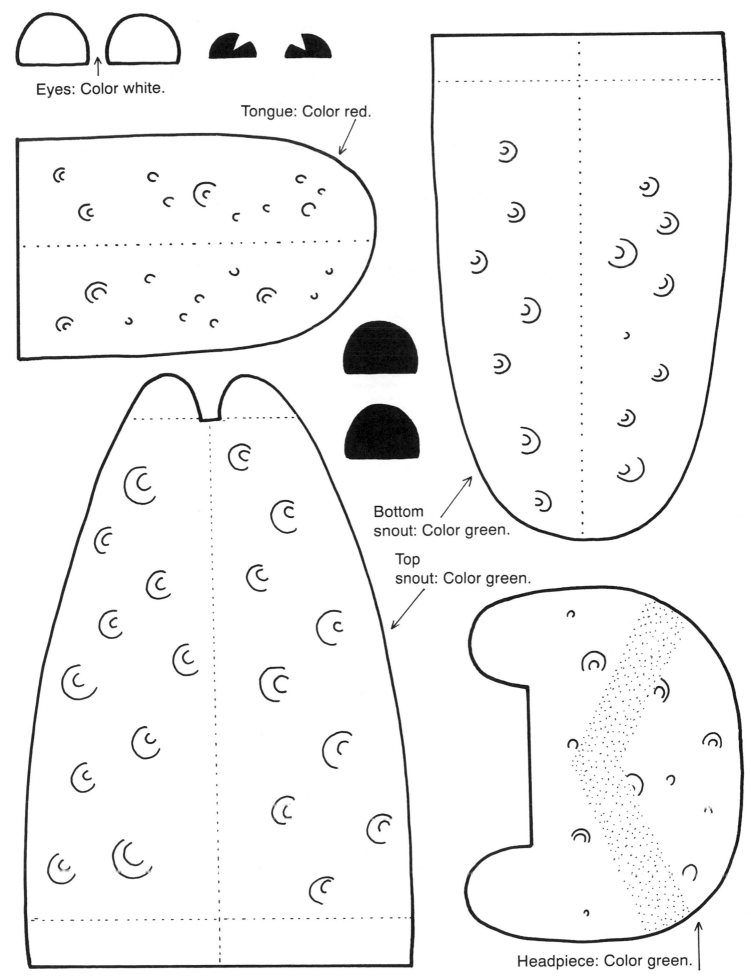

Eyes: Color white.

Tongue: Color red.

Bottom snout: Color green.

Top snout: Color green.

Headpiece: Color green.

105

Color teeth white.

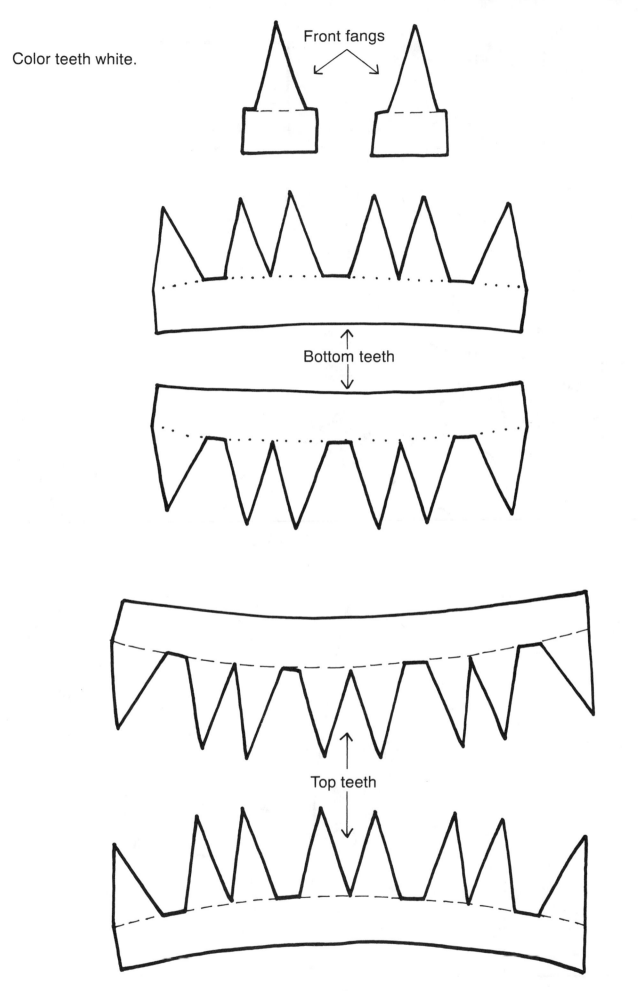

Front fangs

Bottom teeth

Top teeth

106

GA1412

Art: Make a Paper Bag Puppet
Celebrate Clowns

1. Color clown's face and body.
2. Cut out.
3. Fold paper lunch sack flat.
4. Glue clown's face to the bottom part of the sack.
5. Glue clown's body to the side of the sack. (Be sure to place the body up under the face.)
6. Have students slide their hands into the sacks to make the clowns talk.

107

GA1412

Art: Make a Paper Bag Puppet
Celebrate Columbus

1. Color Columbus' face and body.
2. Cut out.
3. Fold paper lunch sack flat.
4. Glue Columbus' face to the bottom part of the sack.
5. Glue Columbus' body to the side of the sack. (Be sure to place the body up under the face.)
6. Have students slide their hands into the sacks to make Columbus talk.

GA1412

Art: Make a Paper Bag Puppet
Celebrate America—Uncle Sam

1. Color Uncle Sam's face and body.
2. Cut out.
3. Fold paper lunch sack flat.
4. Glue Uncle Sam's face to the bottom part of the sack.
5. Glue Uncle Sam's body to the side of the sack. (Be sure to place the body up under the face.)
6. Have students slide their hands into the sacks to make Uncle Sam talk.

Art: Make a Paper Bag Puppet
Celebrate Thanksgiving–Turkey

1. Color turkey's face, body and tail feathers.
2. Cut out.
3. Fold paper lunch sack flat.
4. Glue turkey's face to the bottom part of the sack.
5. Glue turkey's body to the side of the sack.
6. Glue turkey's tail feathers to the back side of the sack.
7. Have students slide their hands into the sacks to make the turkeys talk.

GA1412

Tail feathers for turkey—
paper bag puppet

111

GA1412

Write a Speech/Give a Speech

On the following pages you will find silly title ideas for writing speeches. Allow students to select their own silly titles and to write silly speeches to be presented to the class.

Remind the students of the following points when they are ready to give their oral presentations.

The speaker should
    1. look at the audience as much as possible.
    2. speak up to be heard.
    3. speak clearly so that the audience can understand every word.
    4. pronounce words distinctly so as to be understood.
    5. stand still so as not to distract the audience from what is being said.

More serious topics to be considered for writing speeches might be:

How to bake a cake	How to groom a dog
How to catch a fish	How to park a car
How to build a fence	How to catch butterflies
How to score a soccer goal	How to clean the chalkboard
How to use a microscope	How to please a substitute teacher
How to wash a car	How to write a speech
How to recycle trash	How to make up a water bed
How to make a touchdown	How to make passing grades
How to prevent cavities	How to iron a shirt
How to be a team player	How to make a new friend

(In addition to each silly speech sheet, you will find a prop sheet. The props may be used by the speech maker to demonstrate what he/she is talking about. Follow the how-to directions on each prop sheet to make the prop.)

GA1412

How to Measure a Giraffe

Written by: _____

113

Props for Speech: Giraffe and Ruler
"How to Measure a Giraffe"

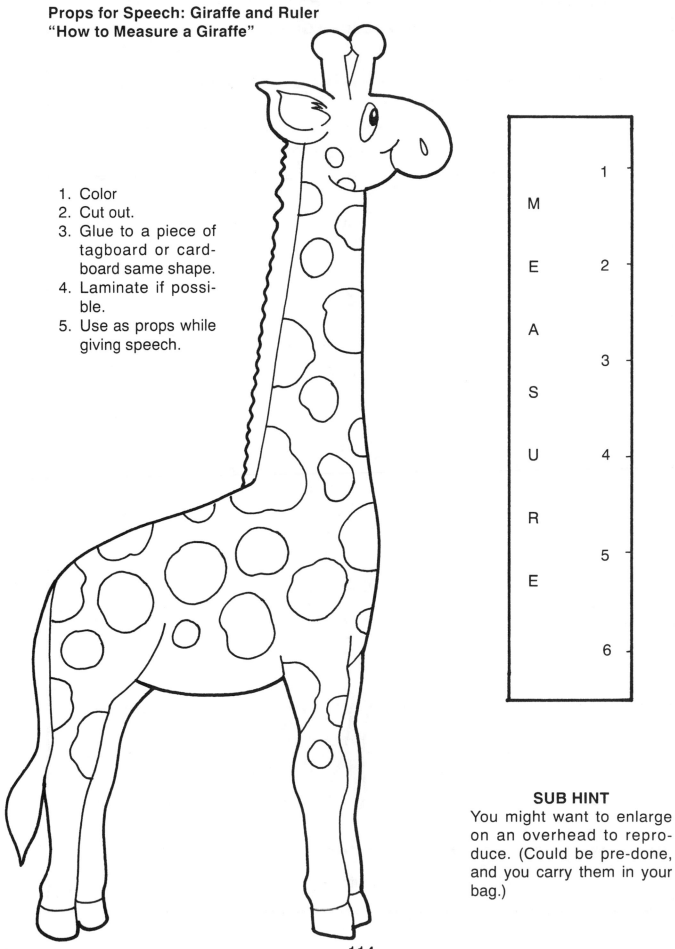

1. Color
2. Cut out.
3. Glue to a piece of tagboard or card-board same shape.
4. Laminate if possi-ble.
5. Use as props while giving speech.

M
E
A
S
U
R
E

1

2

3

4

5

6

SUB HINT
You might want to enlarge on an overhead to repro-duce. (Could be pre-done, and you carry them in your bag.)

GA1412

How to Hide a Hippo

Written by: _____

115

GA1412

Props for Speech: Hippo and Tree, Lion and Zebra
"How to Hide a Hippo"

1. Color.
2. Cut out.
3. Glue to a piece of tagboard or cardboard same shape.

4. Laminate if possible.
5. Use as props while giving speech.

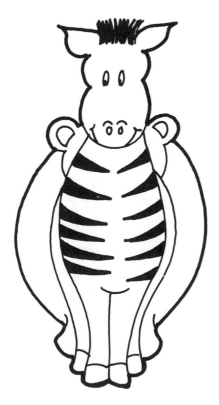

SUB HINT
You might want to enlarge on an overhead to reproduce. (Could be done beforehand and carried in your bag.)

116

GA1412

How to Pet a Crocodile

_____

_____

_____

_____

_____

_____

_____

_____

_____

_____

_____

_____

_____

_____

_____

_____

Written by: _____

GA1412

Props for Speech: Crocodile and Rope
"How to Pet a Crocodile"
1. Color.
2. Cut out.
3. Glue to a piece of tagboard
   or cardboard same shape.
4. Laminate if possible.
5. Use as props while giving speech.

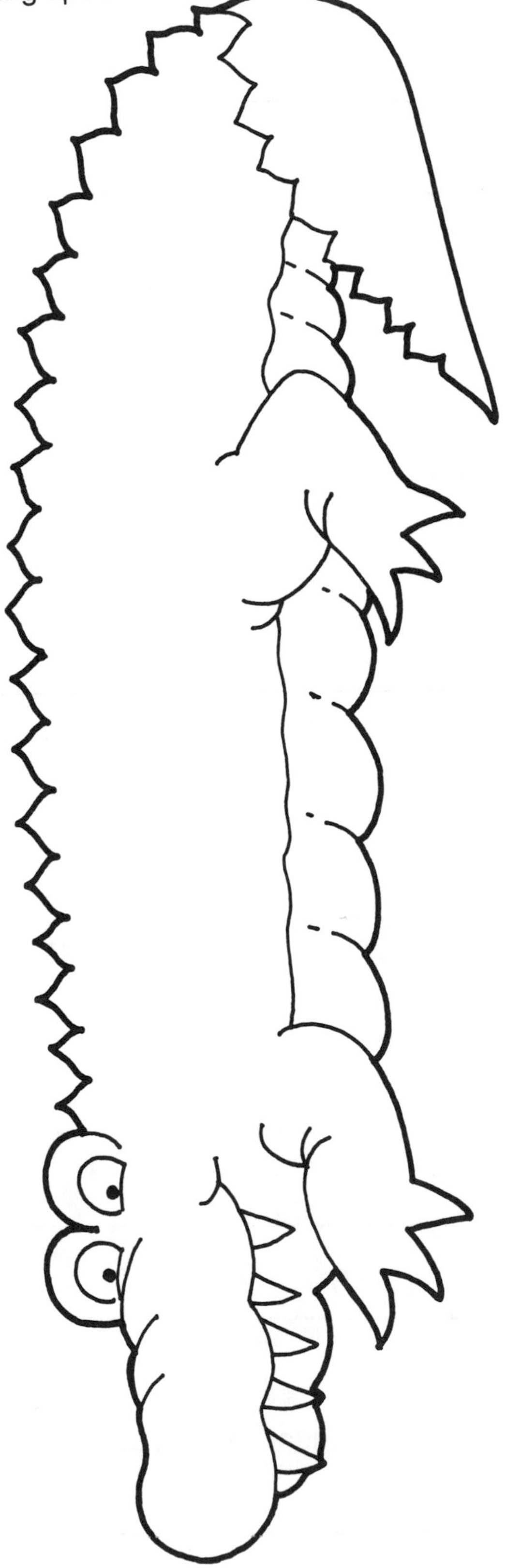

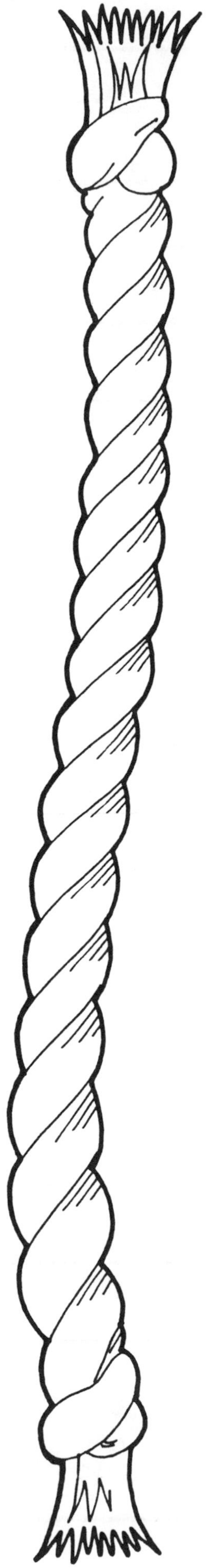

SUB HINT
You might want to en-
large on an overhead to
reproduce. (Could be
done beforehand and
carried in your bag.)

GA1412

How to Dance with a Kangaroo

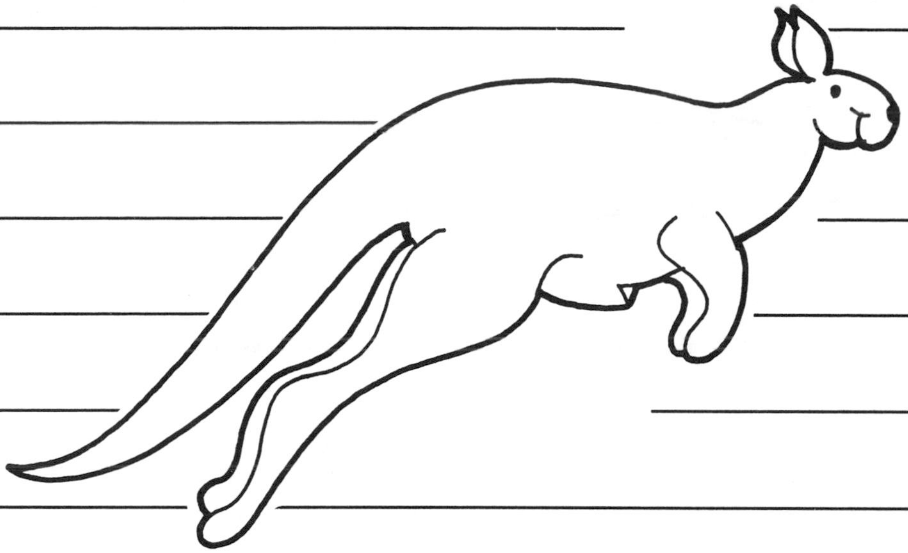

Written by: _____

GA1412

Props for Speech: Kangaroo and Dancing Shoes
"How to Dance with a Kangaroo"

1. Color.
2. Cut out.
3. Glue to a piece of tagboard or cardboard same shape.
4. Laminate if possible.
5. Use as props while giving speech.

SUB HINT

You might want to enlarge on an overhead to reproduce. (Could be done beforehand and carried in your bag.)

How to Hug an Octopus

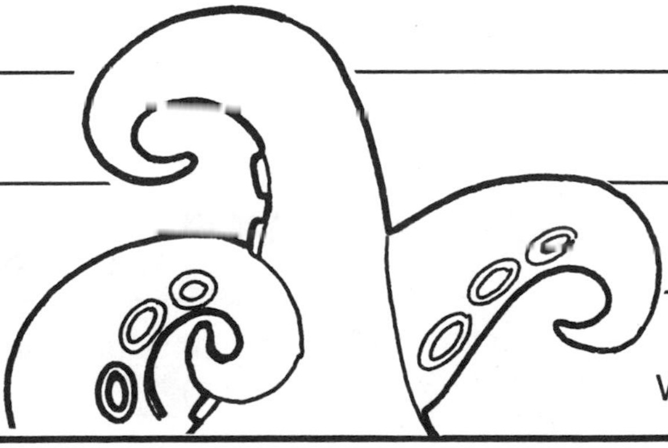

Written by: _____

GA1412

Props for Speech: Octopus and Boy
"How to Hug an Octopus"
1. Color.
2. Cut out.
3. Glue to a piece of tagboard or cardboard same shape.

4. Laminate if possible.
5. Use as props while giving speech.

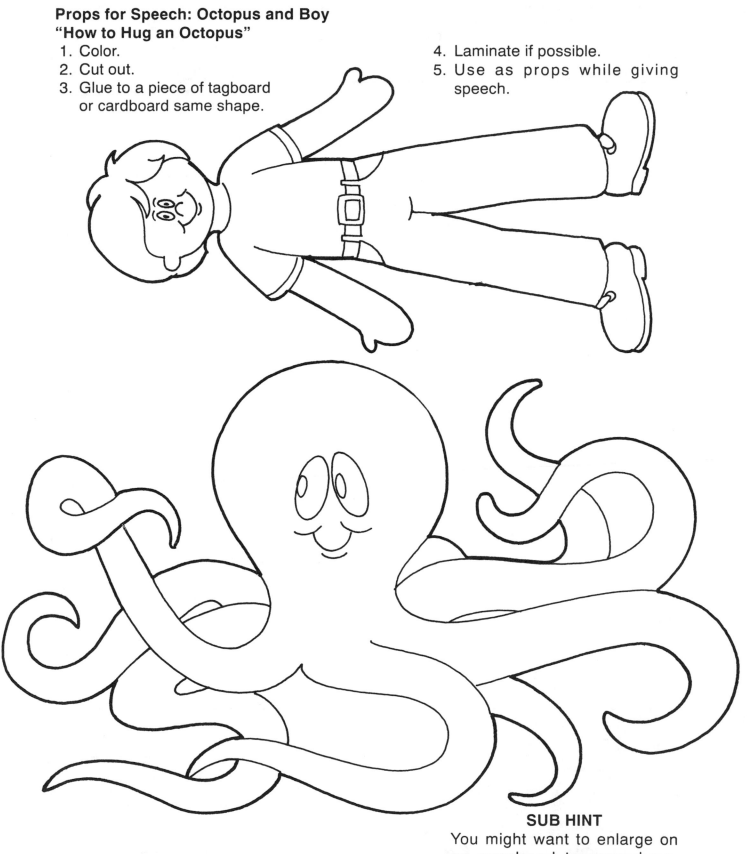

SUB HINT
You might want to enlarge on an overhead to reproduce. (Could be done beforehand and carried in your bag.)

122

GA1412

Make Drug Free Paper Dolls

Use the following pages of paper dolls to instigate a class discussion about saying NO to taking drugs. Stress the paper doll theme, "Dress me cool! I'm drug free!"

Once the paper dolls are colored and cut out, divide the class into small groups. Have the students use the paper dolls to interact scenes in which they say NO to taking drugs.

Discuss ways to say NO to drugs. Some suggestions may be
1. Walk away.

2. Say, "No thanks."

3. Tell them you have better things to do.

4. "Not interested."

5. "My friends don't do drugs, and they don't want me to either."

6. Always work on having a good self-concept. This will keep you from thinking that you need crutches like drugs to make you feel better.

7. Keep your support system of friends nearby.

8. Be selective when making friends. Pick good ones.

9. Be careful not to let yourself get into dangerous situations.

10. Tell them you already have enough problems without adding drugs to the list.

If you as a substitute are able, arrange for the older children to make the paper dolls and then share them with younger children in the school. The older ones can encourage the younger ones to stay away from drugs. If you are not able to make such arrangements, leave a note for the classroom teacher to do so. She will appreciate a fresh idea in the fight against drugs.

GA1412

Drug Free Paper Dolls:
"Dress me cool! I'm drug free!"
1. Color the paper dolls and their clothes.
2. Cut out and dress the dolls in their "drug free" clothes.

124

GA1412

Drug Free Paper Dolls

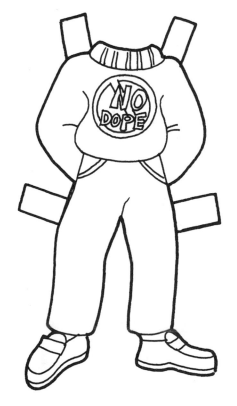

125

Drug Free Paper Dolls

126

Drug Free Paper Dolls

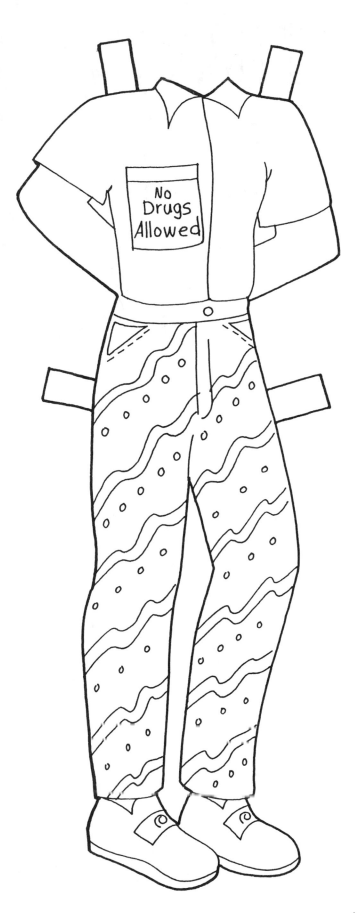

No Drugs Allowed

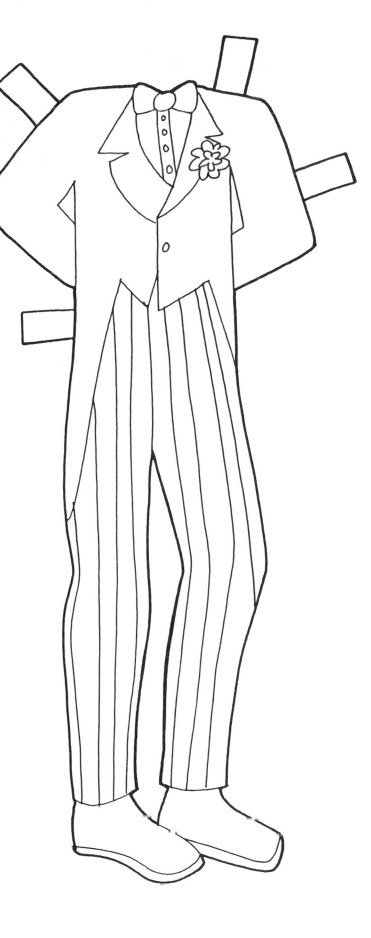

127

GA1412

Drug Free Paper Dolls

128

GA1412

Drug Free Paper Dolls

129

GA1412

Drug Free Paper Dolls

We are proud to say that our family is drug free.

130

GA1412

Drug Free Paper Dolls

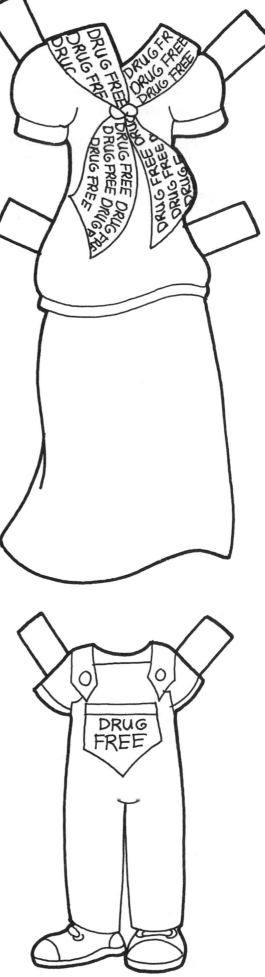

131

GA1412

Write Poetry

Most students will really enjoy writing poetry as long as they understand what is expected of them.

The following seven pages offer suggestions for writing poems that are clear and concise enough for the children to easily be creative.

The poetry suggestions are
1. HAIKU–a three-lined Japanese poem based on word syllables
2. CINQUAIN–a five-lined verse based on word syllables
3. COUPLET–a two-lined verse that rhymes
4. ACROSTIC poem–each letter of a word used as the beginning letter for a line.
5. TONGUE TWISTER–repeating the first letter in each word.
6. a THESAURUS poem–uses words from a thesaurus and their synonyms.
7. a poem about a FRIEND–five lines that follow a specific pattern.

Once you have exhausted these ideas while subbing, just give the students some rhyming word ideas and tell them to write poetry. They love to be creative by playing with rhyming words and writing poetry from scratch.

Some rhyming word ideas are

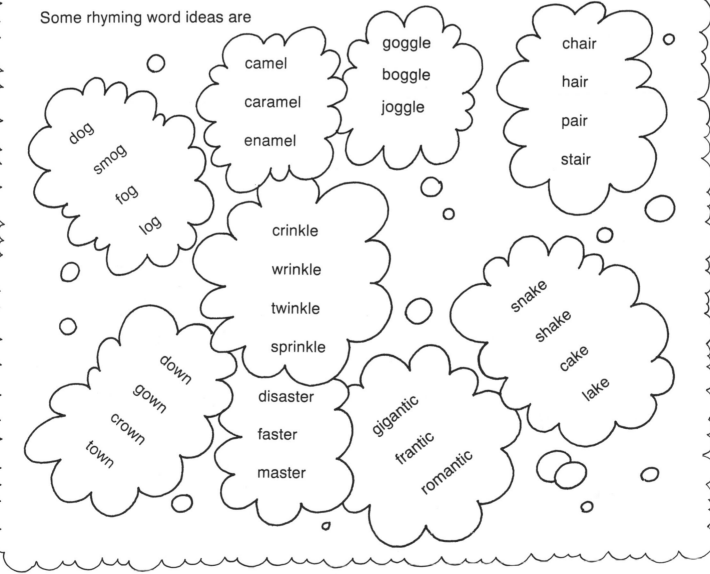

GA1412

Write HAIKU. A haiku is a three-lined, Japanese poem. It does not rhyme, and its lines are made from word syllables. The first line has five syllables, the second has seven, and the third has five. The haiku is usually about nature.

Some examples are
    Elegant petals.
    Nature's breathtaking beauties,
    Soothe our weary hearts.

Old fat, funny frog
Suns himself upon a rock.
Croaks, "Ribbit! Ribbit!'

Write three haiku. Use your own ideas, or choose from the ideas listed below.

Cunning old spider   Crimson red color   Blue ocean waters

    Clumsy young hippo   Serene peaceful place   Cozy warm pillow

Sluggish lazy cat   Shadowy dark jungle   Violent stormy wind

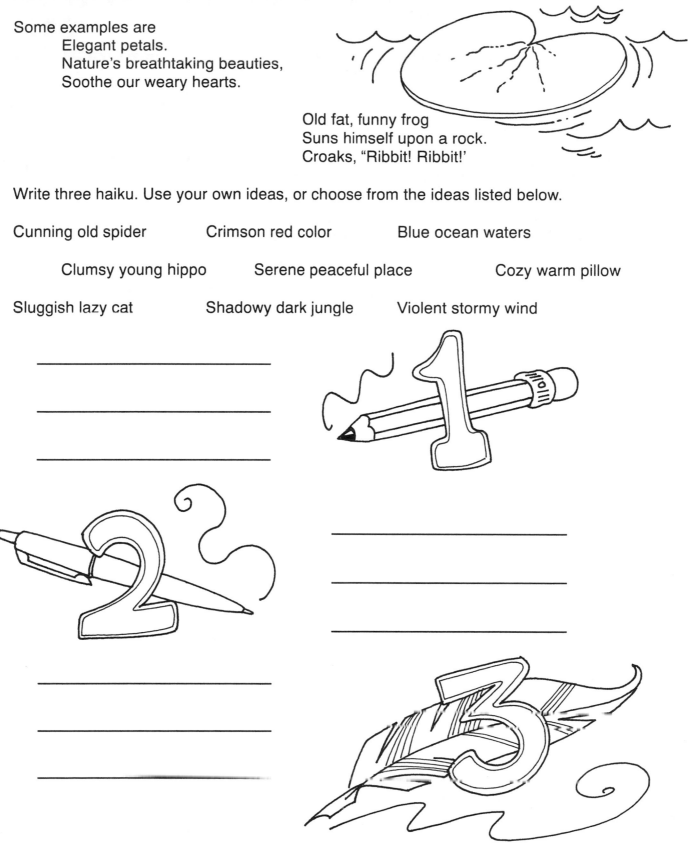

133

GA1412

Write a CINQUAIN. A cinquain is a five-lined verse. It does not rhyme, and its lines are made from word syllables as follows:

First line is one word with two syllables.
Second line is two two-syllable adjectives.
Third line is three *-ing* words with six syllables.
Fourth line is a phrase or sentence with eight syllables that tell about line one.
Fifth line is two syllables that rename the word in line one.

Some examples are

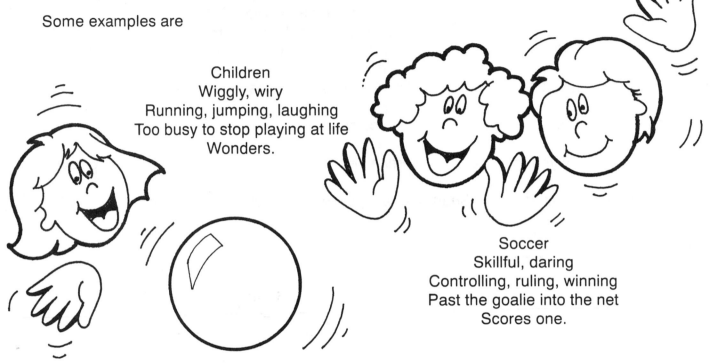

Children
Wiggly, wiry
Running, jumping, laughing
Too busy to stop playing at life
Wonders.

Soccer
Skillful, daring
Controlling, ruling, winning
Past the goalie into the net
Scores one.

Write two cinquains. Use your own ideas, or choose from the ideas listed below.

Summer   Kangaroo   Teacher   Windows

          Books   Family   Wishes   Flowers

Peanut butter   Dreams   Colors   Gardens

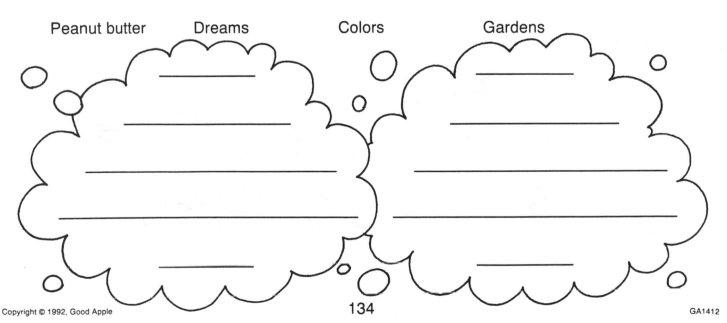

134

GA1412

Write a COUPLET. A couplet is a two-lined verse that rhymes.

Some examples are

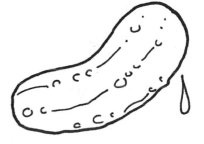

If I just had one tiny nickel,
I could simply buy a pickle.

I would not bother Mister Shark.
He'll be disturbed and make his mark.

Now, you try it. Use the following rhyming words and write a couplet:

clock _____

shock _____

gale _____

whale _____

cool _____

school _____

free _____

bee _____

baboon _____

bassoon _____

house _____

mouse _____

GA1412

Write an ACROSTIC POEM. An acrostic poem is a poem in which each letter of a word is used as the beginning letter for one line of poetry. The lines do not need to rhyme.

Some examples are

Giants
In
Rugged
Africa
Fumble
For
Excellent
Suppers.

Boys will
Always
Suffer,
Even
Bravely
At
Losing their
Last game.

Try writing acrostic poetry on your own by using the words below.

P _____

I _____

Z _____

Z _____

A _____

T _____

E _____

L _____

E _____

V _____

I _____

S _____

C _____

A _____

R _____

T _____

O _____

O _____

N _____

S _____

I _____

O _____

N _____

Or pick your own word. Write an acrostic poem, and illustrate it.

GA1412

Write TONGUE TWISTER POETRY by repeating the first letter in each word of the poem.

Some examples are

Santa's sleigh slid sideways sending snowballs soaring.

Two tiny Tims tried taking toads to town.

Four funny firemen fought fiercely for flaming fires.

Begin by completing these:

Susie Sims smiles _____.

Roosters roar right _____.

Babies bawl badly _____.

Send soiled socks _____.

Nine nasty noses _____.

Now use your own ideas and write tongue twister poetry.

_____

_____

_____

_____

_____

GA1412

Use a THESAURUS to write a poem. A thesaurus is a book of words and their synonyms.

First, decide on an adjective such as lovable, pretty, mean, big, or colorful. Next, look the adjective up in the thesaurus.

On the first line, write the adjective.
On the second line, write two words from the thesaurus that mean the same thing as the adjective.
On the third line, write three words that mean the same.
On the fourth line, write four words that mean the same.
On the fifth line, write a noun that all of the above adjectives describe.

An example is

Lovable
Adorable, dear,
Likeable, enchanting, pleasing,
Sweet, good, warm, tender,
Teddy Bear.

Write your poem here.

_____

_____

_____

_____

Write a poem about a FRIEND. Write five lines that follow this pattern:

Line one—Name your friend.

Line two—Write two adjectives that describe your friend.

Line three—Tell what your friend does.

Line four—Name something your friend enjoys.

Line five—Use another word or phrase to rename your friend.

Some examples are

Ann
Loving, caring,
Teaches children,
Enjoys being with friends,
A good listener.

Kyle
Easy going, untroubled,
Plays football,
Enjoys all sports,
Full of life.

Now, write about your friends.

GA1412

Save the Earth

Our earth is in trouble! It suffers from overcrowded landfills or garbage dumps, contamination from oil spills, polluted waterways and beaches, dirty air and acid rain, the tearing down of our tropical rain forests, and the near expulsion of our endangered animals.

Turn students on to saving the earth and its environment. Make them aware of the problem and what part they might play in solving it. Students can make a difference if they do their part.

All teachers including substitutes can help make students aware. Saving the earth is a problem that belongs to all of us.

Begin by writing for information on ideas to help our environment. First, review the form for writing a business letter. Second, have students select one of the given addresses for environmental organizations. Third, provide the business letter form on the following page, and finally, encourage the students to write for information. The class theme should be "Become aware!"

Addresses:

National Audubon Society
950 Third Avenue
New York, NY 10022

Greenpeace
1436 U Street, N.W.
Washington, D.C. 20009

Sierra Club
730 Polk Street
San Francisco, CA 94109

National Recycling Coalition
1101 30th Street, N.W.
Suite 305
Washington, D.C. 20007

Keep America Beautiful
9 West Broad Street
Stamford, CT 06892

Date
Your address
City, State, Zip

Name of organization
Address
City, State, Zip
Dear Sir,

_____
_____
_____
_____
_____
_____
_____
_____
_____
_____
_____
_____
_____

Sincerely,
Your name

GA1412

Business Letter Form:

_____

_____

_____

_____

_____

_____

_____

_____

_____

_____

_____

_____

_____

_____

_____

_____

_____

_____

_____

GA1412

Make Save the Earth Bookmarks
Use the bookmark over and over. When you finish
with the bookmark, recycle it.
1. Color. 2. Cut out. 3. Pass out to friends.
Encourage everyone to save the earth.

Let me grow, so you can breathe.

RECYCLE

FIX IT   FIX IT

Please—Save the Whales!

GA1412

Make window signs for your car. Tape them facing out so that all those who pass you can read the sign. Spread the word along the highway—SAVE OUR EARTH! SAVE OUR ANIMALS! CUT PLASTIC RINGS.

1. Color.
2. Cut out.
3. Tape two ends of window sign together.
4. Tape in car window facing out for all to see.

GA1412

GA1412

Window Signs

Recycle trash.

1. Color.
2. Cut out.
3. Tape two ends of window sign together.
4. Tape in car window facing out for all to see.

GA1412

146

Save the Earth
Color Sheets: Recycle Trash
1. Copy enough color sheets for a whole class. Carry them in your bag. 2. Have students color to "become aware."

147

1. Copy enough color sheets for a whole class. Carry them in your bag. 2. Have students color to "become aware."

GA1412

Save the Earth:
Color Sheets: Keep the Air Clean
1. Copy enough color sheets for a whole class. Carry them in your bag. 2. Have students color to "become aware."

Keep the Air Clean

GA1412

Make dioramas depicting endangered animals.
Use a shoe box, construction paper, scissors, glue, and the endangered animal patterns found on the following pages.
To make the diorama:

1. Cover the outside of the shoe box with colorful Con-Tact paper.
2. Select an endangered animal pattern. Read about the animal and its habitat.
3. Use construction paper cutouts to create the animal's habitat. Using glue, place the colored endangered animal in place.
4. Display the diorama to make others aware of the plight of these animals.

Hint: This project would be good for a substitute who is planning to be in a classroom for several days. Just ask each student to bring in a shoe box. The other supplies should be available.

GA1412

Endangered Animals

Gray Whale

Grizzly Bear

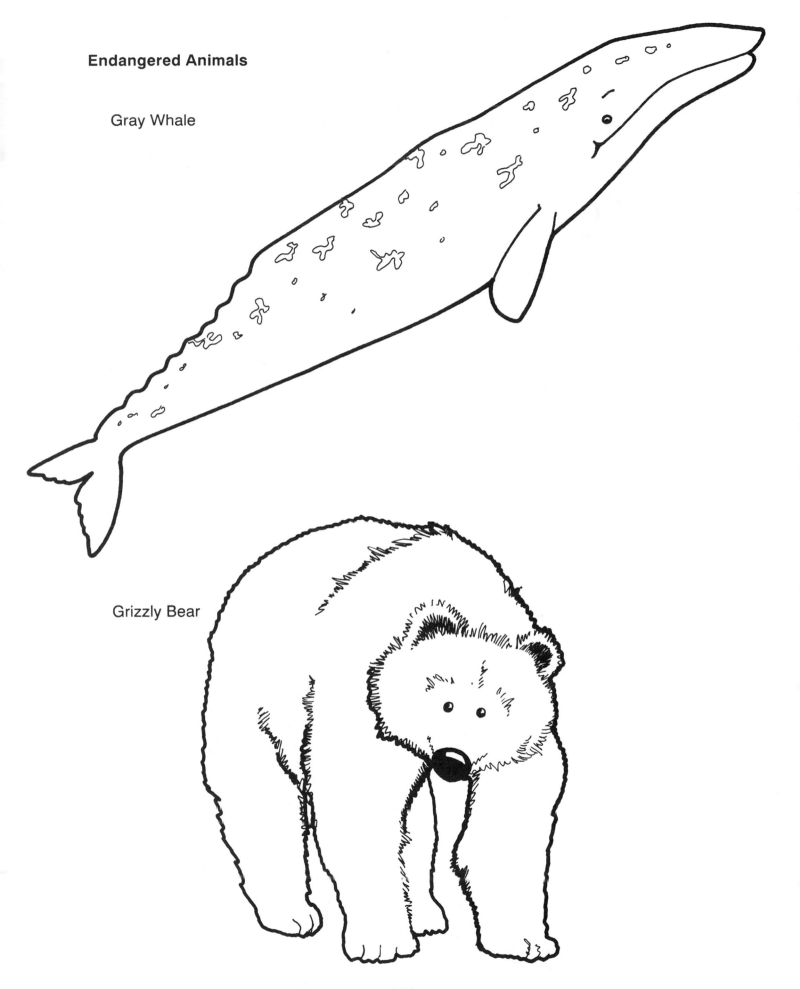

Endangered Animals

Black Rhinoceros

Gorilla

152

GA1412

Endangered Animals

Arizona Trout

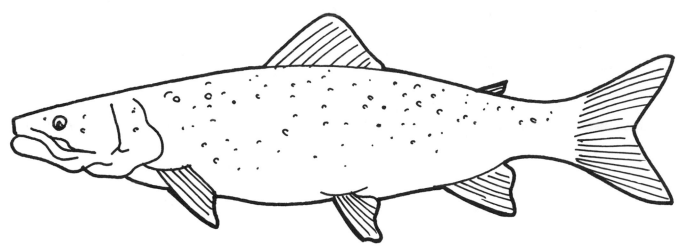

American Crocodile

Write a descriptive paragraph. Provide each student with a picture (magazine, newspaper, etc.) of a pollution problem that faces the earth. Some examples might be stockpiles of garbage, an oil spill, acid rain, pesticide leakage into groundwater, senseless murder of endangered animals, polluted air from smokestacks, animals caught in plastic ring traps, the destruction of our rain forests, and so on.

To write the paragraph:

First, decide what your subject or title will be (Example.: Overcrowded Landfill). Your purpose for writing is to describe a pollution problem that our earth has. Your audience should be the citizens of America.

To write your general impression sentence which will be your topic sentence, look the magazine picture over and write an overall impression of it (Example: The landfills in America are so overcrowded that the day will soon come that we will run out of places to bury our garbage.)

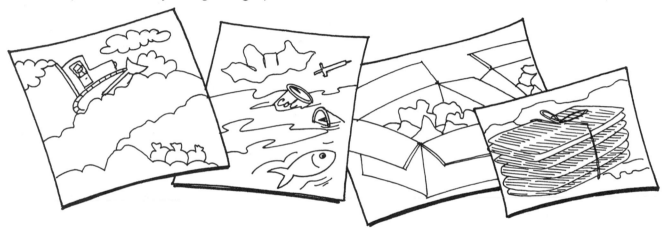

Second, look your picture over and write sensory words that you can imagine as you view the scene.

(Example.:	touch	smell	sight	taste	sound
	slimy	offensive	nasty	does not apply	crunchy

Third, look over your sensory word list and write three to four detail sentences to use in your paragraph. Be sure to use a good supply of the sensory words in your chart.
(Example.: The slimy, offensive garbage overpowers the fresh air and causes me to choke on the smell.)

Finally, write an overall summary sentence to wrap up your paragraph.

Make people aware by running off copies of your paragraphs and by passing them out for all to read.

GA1412

Writing a Descriptive Paragraph

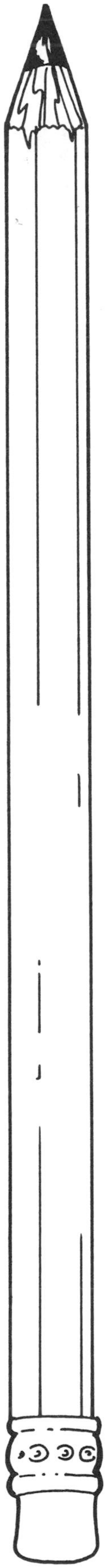

First: Fill in the chart to get you started.

Subject (Title): _____

Purpose of writing: _____

Audience: _____

General impression/Topic sentence: _____

_____

_____

_____

Second: Think of sensory details that might apply to the picture you have to describe.

touch	smell	sight	taste	sound

Third: Write three to four detail sentences using sensory words from the chart above. Choose the best words to express your general impression of the picture to your audience.

_____

_____

_____

_____

GA1412

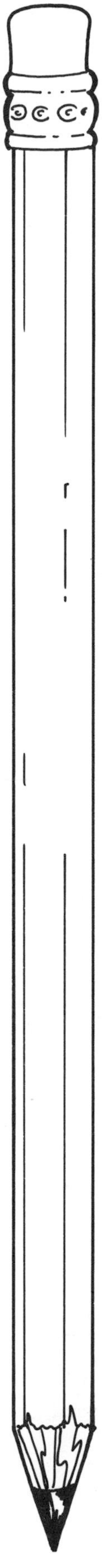

Fourth: Write an overall summary sentence to be used as the closing sentence for your paragraph.

_____

_____

Fifth: Write a rough draft for your descriptive paragraph. Edit your work with a red pen. Then on another sheet of paper, write your final copy.

_____

_____

_____

_____

_____

_____

_____

_____

_____

_____

_____

_____

_____

_____

_____

GA1412